Grilling for Beginners

Learn to Grill Everything with an Easy Grilling Cookbook Filled with Delicious Grilling Recipes

By
BookSumo Press
All rights reserved

Published by
http://www.booksumo.com

Table of Contents

Grilled Salad 7

Tater Tots on the Grill 8

African Rump Steak 9

Mendoza Kabobs 10

Creole Fish 11

Grilled Gazebo Salad 12

Texas Sirloins 13

Miami Café Scallops 14

Southwest Rib-Eye Steaks 15

Laguna Lunch Wraps 16

A Whole Chicken in Belize 17

Persian Fruit Bowls 18

Topped Seafood Tacos 19

Oswego Backyard Bisque 20

Arizona Steak Tacos 21

Jackie's Favorite Fish Tacos 22

Seattle Park Pizza Kitchen 23

Garlicky Fish Griller 24

Bobby's Burgers with the Works 25

Honey Basil Chicken 27

Cuban Style Flanks 28

Homemade Chips for the Summer 29

Grilled Potato Platter 30

Hot Jamaican Filets 31

Endive on the Grill 32

Southwest Sirloin 33

German Pub Food 34

Grandma's Favorite 35

Blackened Italian Tomatoes 36

Saranac Lake Salmon 37

5-Ingredient Salmon 38

Grilled Sausage Sandwiches 39

Hibachi Sirloin 40

Nacho for the Summer 41

Delaware Flat Tortillas 42

Blackened Chicken Cutlets 43

Grilled Bread 44

Maui Night's Dinner 45

Lebanese Burgers with White Sauce 46

Fish Africano 48

French Quarter Muffulettas 49

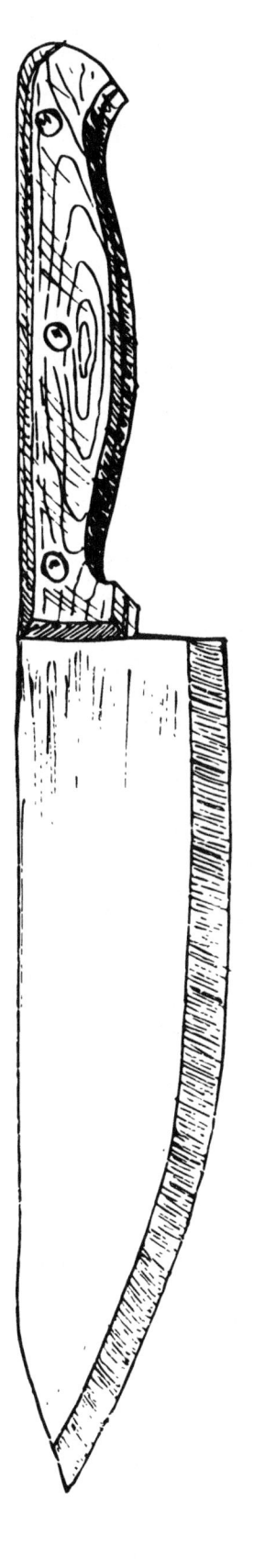

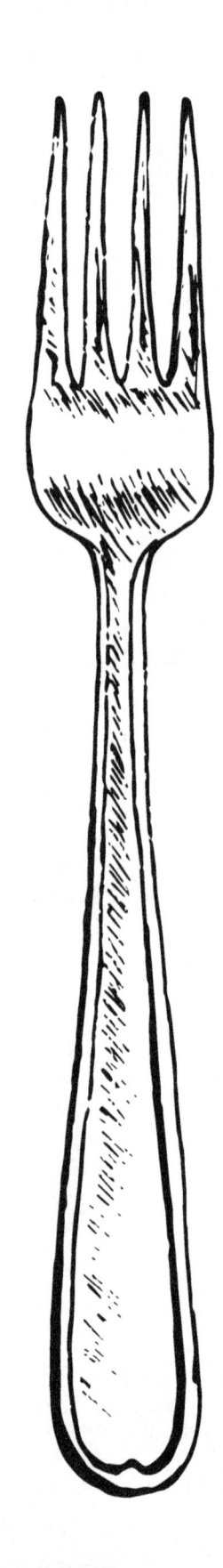

Rosa's Taco Tuesdays 50

5-Ingredient Lamb 51

Wednesday's Linguine Dinner 52

Chicken Supremo 53

How to Grill Shiitake Japanese Style 54

Greek Eggplant Griller 55

Fresh Herbed Flounder 56

Missouri Style T-Bone Steaks 57

Fresh Herbed 'Matoes 58

Asian Style Salmon with Basmati Rice 59

Portuguesa Green Bean Bowls 61

Cookout Pizzas 62

California Food Truck Fajitas 63

Thai Style Tofu 64

Tuscan Potatoes 65

Pasta Salad Penne 66

Pittsburgh Dijon Trout 67

Blackened Grapes 68

Grilled Garlic Bread 69

Megan's Garden Polenta 70

Squash over Pasta 71

Grits in the Summer 72

Persian Style Lamb Chops 73

Spanish Millet Salad 74

Milanese Tomatoes 75

Grilled Fruit Bowls 76

Lighthouse Steaks 77

Greek Style Potatoes 78

Garden Turkey Cutlets 79

Tropical Skewers 80

Grilled Caprese Ciabatta 81

Trout 101 82

How to Grill Collard Greens 83

Simple Salmon 84

House Special Couscous 85

Independence Catfish 86

Chicken Salad Summers 87

Grapefruit Griller 88

Park Ave Fig Kabobs 89

How to Grill Oysters 90

Texan Steak Toppers 91

African Lamb with Chili Sauce 93

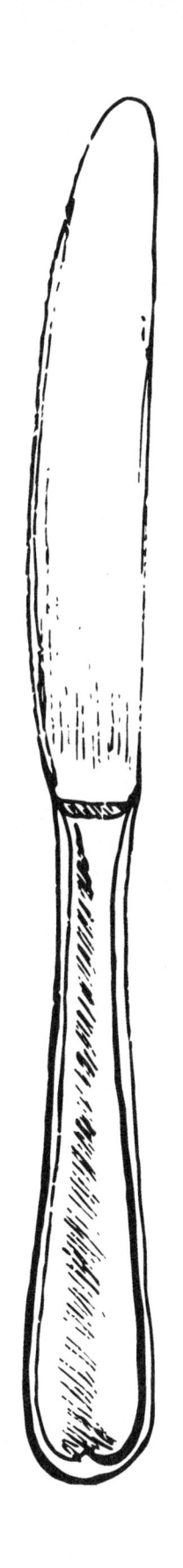

Michelle's Tilapia 94

Mediterrean Lunch Box Salad with Pita 95

American Shrimp Flatbreads 96

Italian Basil Bread 97

Pumpkin Grilled 101 98

Benny's Backyard Beans 99

How to Grill Hash Browns 100

Grilled Salad

🥣 Prep Time: 10 mins
🕐 Total Time: 16 mins

Servings per Recipe: 4
Calories   126.5
Fat   8.4 g
Cholesterol   2.2 mg
Sodium   72.4 mg
Carbohydrates   11.0 g
Protein   4.9 g

Ingredients

- 2 tbsp extra virgin olive oil
- 1 tbsp lemon juice
- 1 small garlic clove, minced
- 1/2 tsp Dijon mustard
- 1/8 tsp Worcestershire sauce
- 1/4 tsp black pepper
- 2 tbsp grated parmesan cheese
- olive oil flavored cooking spray
- 2 romaine lettuce hearts

Directions

1. Get a mixing bowl: Mix in it the oil, lemon juice, garlic, mustard, Worcestershire, and pepper.
2. Add the parmesan cheese and combine them well to make the dressing.
3. Place it in the fridge until ready to serve.
4. Before you do anything, preheat the grill and grease it.
5. Slice the romaine hearts in half lengthwise. Coat them with a cooking spray.
6. Grill them for 3 to 4 min on each side. Serve them warm with the cheese dressing.
7. Enjoy.

TATER TOTS
on the Grill

🥣 Prep Time: 10 mins
🕐 Total Time: 40 mins

Servings per Recipe: 6
Calories   139.3
Fat   3.1 g
Cholesterol   7.6 mg
Sodium   18892.5 mg
Carbohydrates   26.0 g
Protein   3.6 g

Ingredients

Spice Mix
1 C. salt
1/4 C. black pepper
1/4 C. garlic powder
Potatoes

3 golden delight potatoes, sliced into coins
1/4 large sweet onion, sliced
1 1/2 tbsp salted butter, melted
house seasoning

Directions

1. Before you do anything, preheat the grill and grease it.
2. Get a large piece of oil. Fold it in half.
3. Divide between them the potatoes, onion, salt, pepper, garlic powder and melted butter on top.
4. Cover them with a piece of foil. Pinch the edges and seal them.
5. Place it on the grill. Put on the lid and let it cook for 16 to 20 min.
6. Once the time is up, remove the lid and let it cook for an extra 10 to 12 min. Serve it warm.
7. Enjoy.

African Rump Steak

Prep Time: 10 mins
Total Time: 18 mins

Servings per Recipe: 8
Calories   321.4
Fat   17.4 g
Cholesterol   86.4 mg
Sodium   329.1 mg
Carbohydrates   9.4 g
Protein   30.7 g

Ingredients

- 2 1/2 lbs. rump steak
- 1/2 C. chutney
- 1/2 C. ketchup
- 1/4 C. Worcestershire sauce
- 1 tbsp white vinegar
- 3 tbsp apple cider vinegar
- 2 garlic cloves, minced
- 2 onions, sliced
- 1 (8 oz.) cans mushrooms, drained
- salt and pepper

Directions

1. Slice the steak into large chunks. Sprinkle over them some salt and pepper.
2. Get a mixing bowl: Whisk in it the remaining ingredients.
3. Add the steak chunks and toss them to coat. Cover it and let it sit for 60 min.
4. Before you do anything, preheat the grill and grease it.
5. Drain the steaks pieces and grill them for 6 to 10 min on each side. Serve them warm.
6. Enjoy.

MENDOZA
Kabobs

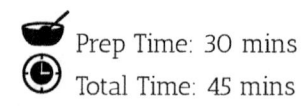

Prep Time: 30 mins
Total Time: 45 mins

Servings per Recipe: 4
Calories 532.5
Fat 40.9 g
Cholesterol 92.8 mg
Sodium 96.2 mg
Carbohydrates 9.7 g
Protein 31.5 g

Ingredients

4 chicken breasts, diced
1/2 red bell pepper, cut into squares
1/2 green bell pepper, cut into squares
2 yellow onions, cut into eighths
1 C. cherry tomatoes
bamboo skewer
1/2 C. oil

3 cloves garlic, chopped
1 tsp paprika
1/2 tsp Mexican oregano
kosher salt
black peppercorns

Directions

1. Before you do anything, preheat the grill and grease it.
2. Get a food processor: Combine in it the Oil, Garlic, Paprika, Oregano, Salt, and Peppercorns.
3. Process them several times until they become smooth to make the marinade.
4. Get a large mixing bowl: Combine in it the chicken dices with marinade.
5. Cover the bowl and let it sit for at least 20 min.
6. Before you do anything else, preheat the grill and grease it.
7. Thread the chicken dices with onion, peppers, and cherry tomatoes onto skewers while alternating between them.
8. Grill them for 8 to 10 min on each side. Serve them warm.
9. Enjoy.

Creole Fish

Prep Time: 5 mins
Total Time: 15 mins

Servings per Recipe: 6
Calories   192.6
Fat   9.4 g
Cholesterol   87.4 mg
Sodium   155.9 mg
Carbohydrates   0.9 g
Protein   24.3 g

Ingredients

- 1 tsp lemon pepper seasoning
- 1 tsp white pepper
- 1 tsp Creole seasoning
- 4 catfish fillets
- 2 tbsp lemon juice
- lemon wedge

Directions

1. Get a mixing bowl: Stir in it the fish seasoning with lemon pepper seasoning, white pepper, and creole seasoning.
2. Massage the mixture into the catfish fillets.
3. Before you do anything, preheat the grill and grease it.
4. Grill the fish fillets for 5 to 6 min on each side. Serve them warm.
5. Enjoy.

GRILLED
Gazebo Salad

🥣 Prep Time: 15 mins
🕐 Total Time: 25 mins

Servings per Recipe: 8
Calories   336.1
Fat   18.2 g
Cholesterol   29.5 mg
Sodium   428.5 mg
Carbohydrates   32.6 g
Protein   10.7 g

Ingredients

Vegetables
4 cloves roasted garlic, minced
1 red pepper, quartered
1 portabella mushroom
1 onion, sliced
1 zucchini, sliced into 4 long strips
3 tbsp olive oil
3 tbsp balsamic vinegar
tsp Italian seasoning
Dressing
2 cloves garlic, minced

1/4 C. olive oil
1/8 C. balsamic vinegar
1 sprig rosemary, stem discarded leaves chopped
Salad
16 oz. cheese tortellini
1/2 C. provolone cheese, diced
4 oz. black olives
salt and pepper

Directions

1. Get a large zip lock bag: Combine in it the veggies with oil, vinegar, and Italian seasoning.
2. Seal the bag and let them sit for 60 min in the fridge.
3. Before you do anything, preheat the grill and grease it.
4. Grill the veggies for 3 to 4 min on each side.
5. Place them aside to cool down for a bit. Dice them.
6. Get a food processor: Combine in it the salad dressing ingredients. Blend them smooth.
7. Get a large mixing bowl: Combine in it the grilled veggies with tortellini, cheese, olives, dressing, a pinch of salt and pepper.
8. Stir them to coat. Adjust the seasoning of your salad then serve it with extra toppings of your choice.
9. Enjoy.

Texas Sirloins

Prep Time: 5 mins
Total Time: 24 hrs 5 mins

Servings per Recipe: 2
Calories   1253.6
Fat   91.4 g
Cholesterol   333.2 mg
Sodium   820.8 mg
Carbohydrates   5.5 g
Protein   96.2 g

Ingredients

- 1 1/2 lbs. top sirloin steaks
- 2 tbsp vegetable oil
- 1 tsp dried oregano leaves
- 1 tsp garlic powder
- 1/2 tsp salt
- 1 tsp ground pepper
- 1/4 C. orange juice
- 2 tsp cider vinegar

Directions

1. Get a mixing bowl: Toss in it all the ingredients.
2. Cover the bowl and let it sit overnight.
3. Before you do anything, preheat the grill and grease it.
4. Drain the steaks and grill them for 10 to 14 min on each side. Serve them warm.
5. Enjoy.

MIAMI
Café Scallops

Prep Time: 15 mins
Total Time: 20 mins

Servings per Recipe: 2
Calories	123.1
Fat	0.9 g
Cholesterol	41.1 mg
Sodium	1544.6 mg
Carbohydrates	6.6 g
Protein	20.8 g

Ingredients

12 oz. frozen sea scallops, thawed and drained
1 tsp dried thyme
1 tsp ground black pepper
1 tsp kosher salt
1 tsp lime zest

Directions

1. Soak the bamboo skewers in water for 10 to 20 min.
2. Drain them and thread onto them the scallops.
3. Get a mixing bowl: Mix in it the rest of the ingredients. Massage the mixture gently into the scallops.
4. Before you do anything, preheat the grill and grease it.
5. Grill the scallop skewers for 2 to 4 min on each side. Serve them warm.
6. Enjoy.

Southwest Rib-Eye Steaks

Prep Time: 2 hrs 10 mins
Total Time: 2 hrs 25 mins

Servings per Recipe: 6
Calories   379.4
Fat   37.4 g
Cholesterol   0.0 mg
Sodium   1191.8 mg
Carbohydrates   11.8 g
Protein   2.7 g

Ingredients

4 oz. bunch flat leaf parsley, stemmed, chopped
4 oz. bunch cilantro, chopped
3 garlic cloves, minced
2 tbsp ground cumin
1 tbsp ground coriander
2 tbsp sweet paprika
1 tsp smoked paprika
1 tsp cayenne pepper
1 pinch saffron thread
1/4 C. lemon juice
1 C. olive oil
1 tbsp kosher salt
6 boneless rib-eye steaks, excess fat trimmed, cubed
2 red onions, chopped
2 red bell peppers, chopped

Directions

1. Get a blender: Place in it the parsley with cilantro, garlic, cumin, coriander, paprika, cayenne, and saffron.
2. Process them until them until they become smooth.
3. Combine in the olive oil with lemon juice and salt. Blend them smooth to make the marinade.
4. Get a mixing bowl: Stir in it the steak cubes with half of the marinade.
5. Cover the bowl and let it sit in the fridge for 120 min.
6. Before you do anything, preheat the grill and grease it.
7. Thread the steak cubes with onion and peppers onto skewers while alternating between them.
8. Grill them for 7 to 8 min on each side.
9. Serve your steak skewers warm with the remaining marinade.
10. Enjoy.

LAGUNA
Lunch Wraps

Prep Time: 10 mins
Total Time: 25 mins

Servings per Recipe: 6
Calories   538.4
Fat   25.2 g
Cholesterol   110.0 mg
Sodium   750.5 mg
Carbohydrates   43.0 g
Protein   34.7 g

Ingredients

2 tbsp olive oil
8 boneless skinless chicken thighs
1 sweet onion
1 cucumber
8 oz. Monterey jack and cheddar cheese blend
6 slices turkey bacon

16 oz. shredded lettuce
ranch salad dressing
6 (10 inches) flour tortillas
1 lime

Directions

1. Place a pan over medium heat. Heat in it the oil.
2. Slice the chicken thighs into strips. Season them with a pinch of salt and pepper.
3. Cook them in the hot oil for 8 to 10 min until they are done. Drain them and place them aside.
4. Place a small pan over medium heat. Cook in it the bacon until it becomes crisp.
5. Drain it and place it aside.
6. Heat the tortillas in a pan or microwave. Lay them on a cutting board.
7. Top them with ranch, lettuce, cucumbers, onion, bacon, cheese.
8. Arrange the chicken strips on top followed by some lime juice.
9. Wrap the tortillas and toast them on a grill or pan grill for 2 to 3 min on each side. Serve them warm.
10. Enjoy.

A Whole Chicken in Belize

Prep Time: 10 mins
Total Time: 45 mins

Servings per Recipe: 4
Calories   779.1
Fat   56.7 g
Cholesterol   243.8 mg
Sodium   1569.3 mg
Carbohydrates   4.0 g
Protein   60.3 g

Ingredients

1/3 C. soy sauce
2 tbsp lime juice
5 garlic cloves
2 tsp ground cumin
1 tsp paprika
1/2 tsp dried oregano
1 tbsp vegetable oil
1 whole chicken, quartered

Directions

1. Get a food processor: Combine in it the soy sauce, lime juice, garlic, cumin, paprika, oregano, 1/2 tsp pepper, and oil.
2. Get a large zip lock bag: place in it the chicken pieces. Pour over it the marinade.
3. Seal the bag and let it sit in the fridge for 7 h to 26 h.
4. Before you do anything, preheat the grill and grease it.
5. Grill the chicken pieces for 15 to 18 min on each side. Serve them warm.
6. Enjoy.

PERSIAN
Fruit Bowls

🥣 Prep Time: 10 mins
🕐 Total Time: 13 mins

Servings per Recipe: 6
Calories 249.6
Fat 8.5 g
Cholesterol 21.0 mg
Sodium 76.0 mg
Carbohydrates 39.3 g
Protein 7.6 g

Ingredients

1/3 C. honey
1 tbsp water
2 tsp orange blossom water
9 medium figs, stems trimmed and halved lengthwise
1-quart yogurt
1/3 C. pistachios, roasted, salted and chopped

Directions

1. Before you do anything, preheat the grill and grease it.
2. Get a mixing bowl: Whisk in it the honey, water, and orange blossom water.
3. Before you do anything, preheat the grill and grease it.
4. Place the figs on a baking tray. Coat them with the honey mixture.
5. Lay them on the grill and put on the lid.
6. Let them cook for 2 to 3 min while basting them with the leftover honey mixture.
7. Turn over the figs and cook them for an extra 1 to 2 min.
8. Garnish your grilled figs with pistachios. Serve them with some ice cream.
9. Enjoy

Topped Seafood Tacos

🥣 Prep Time: 3 mins
🕐 Total Time: 10 mins

Servings per Recipe: 2
Calories   316.4
Fat   18.8 g
Cholesterol   7.2 mg
Sodium   152.2 mg
Carbohydrates   32.3 g
Protein   8.3 g

Ingredients

Sauce
1 large avocado, chopped
1/2 C. water
1/4 C. loosely packed cilantro
1/2-1 large pickled jalapeno pepper, seeded
1 tbsp fresh limes
1 large garlic clove
kosher salt
black pepper
Marinade
1 tbsp olive oil
1/2 limes, zest
1 tbsp limes
1 garlic clove, minced
kosher salt
pepper
Tacos
4 -6 large sea scallops
olive oil
1/2 C. green cabbage, sliced
1/4 C. red onion, sliced
1 -1 1/2 tbsp cilantro, chopped
4 corn tortillas

Directions

1. Get a food processor: Combine it all the sauce ingredients.
2. Blend them smooth to make the sauce. Get a mixing bowl: Whisk in it the marinade ingredients.
3. Cut each scallop in half. Stir into it into the marinade. Put on the lid and chill it in the fridge for 16 min.
4. Get a mixing bowl: Combine in it the cabbage with onion and cilantro.
5. Place a large pan over medium heat. Hat in it the olive oil.
6. Drain the scallops from the marinade. Cook them in the hot oil for 40 sec to 1 min on each side.
7. Heat the tortillas in a pan or a microwave. Place them on serving plates.
8. Top each one of them with the cabbage salad, scallops, and avocado sauce.
9. Wrap your tortillas then toast them in a grill pan or a grill.
10. Serve them warm.
11. Enjoy.

OSWEGO
Backyard Bisque

Prep Time: 15 mins
Total Time: 50 mins

Servings per Recipe: 4
Calories   335.8
Fat   27.2 g
Cholesterol   81.5 mg
Sodium   496.3 mg
Carbohydrates   18.8 g
Protein   8.3 g

Ingredients

8 large ripe yellow tomatoes
1 tbsp olive oil
1 medium red onion, chopped
2 - 3 C. chicken broth
1 tsp granulated sugar
1 C. heavy cream

kosher salt & ground black pepper
1/4 C. chopped mint

Directions

1. Before you do anything, preheat the grill and grease it.
2. Grill in it the tomatoes for 8 to 12 min. Place them aside to lose heat for a while.
3. Peel them and chop them.
4. Place a large stew pot over medium heat. Heat in it the oil.
5. Cook in it the onion for 8 min. Add the chopped tomatoes with broth and sugar.
6. Turn up the heat and cook them until they start boiling.
7. Lower the heat to medium heat. Cook them for 22 min.
8. Once the time is up, turn off the heat and let it cool down for a while.
9. Get a food processor: Pour in it the tomato mixture. Blend them smooth.
10. Pour the mixture back into the pot. Add to it the heavy cream. Heat it for a few minutes.
11. Adjust the seasoning of your soup then serve it warm.
12. Enjoy.

Arizona Steak Tacos

Prep Time: 15 mins
Total Time: 30 mins

Servings per Recipe: 4
Calories   536.3
Fat   33.7 g
Cholesterol   102.2 mg
Sodium   317.9 mg
Carbohydrates   22.8 g
Protein   35.9 g

Ingredients

1 lb. flank steak, trimmed
3/4 lb. white mushroom
1 bell pepper, quartered
1 onion, sliced crosswise
3 tbsp extra virgin olive oil
salt and pepper

8 taco shells
1 C. shredded Monterey jack cheese

Directions

1. Before you do anything, preheat the grill and grease it.
2. Spread the steak, mushrooms, bell pepper and onion.
3. Add to them the olive oil with a pinch of salt and pepper. Toss them to coat.
4. Arrange the steak with veggies on the grill. Let them cook for 6 to 8 min on each side.
5. Allow them to cool down for a while. Cut the steaks into strips.
6. Arrange the grilled veggies with steak slices in taco shells.
7. Top them with cheese then serve them.
8. Enjoy.

JACKIE'S
Favorite Fish Tacos

Prep Time: 15 mins
Total Time: 35 mins

Servings per Recipe: 4
Calories   256.6
Fat   3.9 g
Cholesterol   70.8 mg
Sodium   533.5 mg
Carbohydrates   25.1 g
Protein   31.8 g

Ingredients

2 slices of white onions
1 (8 oz.) packages mini sweet bell peppers
3/4 tsp salt, divided
1/2 tsp ground black pepper, divided
4 (5 oz.) tilapia fillets

8 (6 inches) corn tortillas
1 small jalapeno pepper, sliced
8 lime wedges

Directions

1. Before you do anything, preheat the grill and grease it.
2. Layover it in the onion slices with peppers. Cook them for 5 to 6 min on each side.
3. Once the time is up, let them rest for 6 min.
4. Cut the peppers and onions into slices.
5. Season them with 1/4 tsp salt, and 1/8 tsp black pepper. Place them aside.
6. Season the fish fillets with the remaining salt and pepper.
7. Grill them for 3 to 4 min on each side.
8. Heat the tortillas in a pan or a microwave.
9. Arrange on them the onion, peppers and fish fillets. Serve them with some lime wedges.
10. Enjoy.

Seattle Park Pizza Kitchen

Prep Time: 20 mins
Total Time: 35 mins

Servings per Recipe: 6
Calories   153.3
Fat   9.5 g
Cholesterol   35.6 mg
Sodium   437.6 mg
Carbohydrates   5.3 g
Protein   11.7 g

Ingredients

12 inches pizza crusts, prebaked
1/2 tsp olive oil
2/3 C. spaghetti sauce
2 plum tomatoes, sliced
1/4 C. mushrooms, sliced
1/4 C. water-packed artichoke hearts, rinsed, drained and chopped
2 tbsp sliced ripe olives
1 C. part-skim mozzarella cheese, shredded
1/2 C. feta cheese, crumbled tomato and basil
1 1/2 tsp basil, minced
1 1/2 tsp rosemary, minced, crushed
1 1/2 tsp chives, minced

Directions

1. Before you do anything, preheat the grill and grease it.
2. Coat the pizza crust with 1/2 tsp of olive oil.
3. Top it with the spaghetti sauce followed by tomatoes, mushrooms, artichokes, and olives.
4. Top them with mozzarella cheese, and feta cheese. Season them with a pinch of salt and pepper.
5. Place the pizza on the grill and put on the lid. Let it cook for 10 to 14 min.
6. Top it with basil, rosemary, and chives. Place it aside to lose heat for a while then serve it.
7. Enjoy.

GARLICKY
Fish Griller

Prep Time: 5 mins
Total Time: 20 mins

Servings per Recipe: 4
Calories   261.3
Fat   28.7 g
Cholesterol   0.0 mg
Sodium   146.3 mg
Carbohydrates   2.4 g
Protein   0.1 g

Ingredients

4 fish steaks
1/2 tbsp olive oil
lemon juice
1 tbsp Greek oregano, chopped
 salt
Dressing

2 lemons, juice
1/2 C. extra-virgin olive oil
1 pinch sea salt
1 garlic clove

Directions

1. Before you do anything, preheat the grill and grease it.
2. Coat the fish steaks with olive oil and lemon juice.
3. Season them with oregano, a pinch of salt and pepper.
4. Grill them for 5 to 7 min on each side.
5. Get a blender: Combine in it the dressing ingredients. Blend them smooth.
6. Drizzle the dressing over the fish steaks then serve them.
7. Enjoy.

Bobby's Burgers with the Works

Prep Time: 20 mins
Total Time: 30 mins

Servings per Recipe: 4
Calories   531.9
Fat   36.2 g
Cholesterol   146.2 mg
Sodium   688.0 mg
Carbohydrates   12.1 g
Protein   41.6 g

Ingredients

Relish
1 poblano chile, grilled, peeled, seeded, and chopped
2 medium dill pickle, chopped
1 small red onion, chopped
1/4 C. lime juice
1 tsp honey
2 tbsp chopped cilantro leaves
1/4 tsp ground black pepper
Mayo
1/2 ripe avocado, peeled and chopped
1/4 C. mayonnaise
1 tbsp fresh lime juice
2 garlic cloves, chopped
1/2 tsp ground cumin
1/4 tsp kosher salt
1/4 tsp ground black pepper
Burgers
1 1/2 lbs. ground turkey, lean
2 tbsp canola oil
1/2 tsp kosher salt
1/2 tsp ground black pepper
4 slices Monterey jack cheese

Directions

1. To prepare the relish:
2. Get a mixing bowl: Combine in it all the relish ingredients.
3. Cover it and let it sit for at least 60 min in the fridge.
4. To prepare the avocado mayo:
5. Get a blender: Combine in it all the mayo ingredients. Blend them smooth.
6. To prepare the burgers:
7. Before you do anything, preheat the grill and grease it.
8. Season the turkey meat with a pinch of salt and pepper. Shape it into 4 patties.
9. Coat them with oil then grill them for 4 to 5 min on each side.
10. Top them with cheese and let them cook for an extra minute.
11. Allow the burgers to rest for 4 to 5 min. Place them on the bottom buns and top them with relish.

12. Drizzle over them the avocado mayo then cover them with the top buns. Serve them warm.
13. Enjoy.

Honey Basil Chicken

Prep Time: 6 mins
Total Time: 22 mins

Servings per Recipe: 4
Calories	247.4
Fat	5.7 g
Cholesterol	108.9 mg
Sodium	267.3 mg
Carbohydrates	9.6 g
Protein	37.6 g

Ingredients

- 3 tbsp balsamic vinegar
- 1 tbsp Dijon mustard
- 1 tbsp honey
- 2 garlic cloves, minced
- 1 1/2 lbs. boneless skinless chicken breasts
- 1 C. basil leaf, chopped
- 4 C. baby arugula, chopped
- 1/4 C. sun-dried tomato packed in oil, chopped

Directions

1. To prepare the marinade:
2. Place a heavy saucepan over medium heat. Combine in it the vinegar, mustard, honey, garlic, pepper, and oil. Heat it until it starts boiling. Lower the heat and let it simmer for 4 to 6 min.
3. Before you do anything, preheat the grill and grease it.
4. Place the chicken breasts between 2 pieces of a plastic wrap.
5. Use a meat tenderizer to flatten them until they become 1/2 inch thick. Season the chicken breasts with a pinch of salt and pepper.
6. Grill them for 4 to 6 min on each side. Place them aside and let rest for 5 min. Cut them into strips.
7. Get a large mixing bowl: Combine in it the chicken strips with the heated marinade.
8. Stir them to coat and season them with a pinch of salt and pepper.
9. Arrange the basil with arugula and sun-dried tomatoes on a serving plate.
10. Layover them the chicken mixture. Serve them immediately.
11. Enjoy.

CUBAN STYLE
Flanks

🥣 Prep Time: 6 hrs
🕐 Total Time: 6 hrs 20 mins

Servings per Recipe: 8
Calories   293.4
Fat   12.9 g
Cholesterol   46.4 mg
Sodium   745.9 mg
Carbohydrates   19.2 g
Protein   25.4 g

Ingredients

2/3 C. reduced sugar orange marmalade
1/3 C. soy sauce
1/3 C. lemon juice
2 tbsp canola oil
2 lbs. flank steaks

Directions

1. Get a mixing bowl: Whisk in it the marmalade with soy sauce, lemon juice, and canola oil to make the marinade.
2. Get a large zip lock bag: Place in it the steaks then season them with a pinch of salt and pepper.
3. Pour over them the marinade. Seal the bag and let it sit for 7 to 9 h in the fridge.
4. Before you do anything else, preheat the grill and grease it.
5. Drain the steaks and grill them for 5 to 7 min on each side. Serve them warm.
6. Enjoy.

Homemade Chips for the Summer

Prep Time: 5 mins
Total Time: 10 mins

Servings per Recipe: 6
Calories   142.1
Fat   7.1 g
Cholesterol   0.0 mg
Sodium   160.9 mg
Carbohydrates   16.7 g
Protein   2.7 g

Ingredients

- 3 large pita bread
- 3 tbsp olive oil, extra-virgin
- 1 tbsp sesame seeds

Directions

1. Before you do anything, preheat the grill and grease it.
2. Slice each pita bread into 6 pieces.
3. Coat them with oil and place them on the grill. Sprinkle over them the sesame seeds.
4. Let them cook for 1 to 2 min on each side.
5. Allow them to cool down for a while then serve them.
6. Enjoy.

GRILLED
Potato Platter

🥣 Prep Time: 10 mins
🕐 Total Time: 25 mins

Servings per Recipe: 4
Calories 87.1
Fat 1.2 g
Cholesterol 0.0 mg
Sodium 21.9 mg
Carbohydrates 17.9 g
Protein 1.6 g

Ingredients

1 russet potato, sliced into 8 wedges
1 sweet potato, cut into 8 wedges
1/3 C. lemonade
1 tsp olive oil
1 chipotle chile in adobo, minced
salt
fresh cracked pepper

Directions

1. Before you do anything, preheat the grill.
2. Get an aluminum roasting pan: Combine in it the potatoes with lemonade, olive oil, chile a pinch of salt and pepper.
3. Cover it and place it over the grill. Let them cook for 10 to 14 min until the potatoes become soft.
4. Serve them warm.
5. Enjoy.

Hot Jamaican Filets

Prep Time: 1 hr 5 mins
Total Time: 1 hr 11 mins

Servings per Recipe: 4
Calories	258.0
Fat	8.3 g
Cholesterol	99.0 mg
Sodium	142.1 mg
Carbohydrates	2.2 g
Protein	41.4 g

Ingredients

- 2 tbsp olive oil
- 2 garlic cloves, minced
- 1 1/2 tbsp lime juice
- 1 tbsp fresh ginger, minced
- 1 scotch bonnet pepper, seeded and sliced
- 4 fish fillets
- salt
- black pepper

Directions

1. Get a mixing bowl: Whisk in it the oil, garlic, lime juice, ginger, and scotch bonnet.
2. Add the fish fillets and stir them to coat. Cover the bowl and let it sit for 60 min in the fridge.
3. Before you do anything, preheat the grill and grease it.
4. Drain the fish fillets. Sprinkle over them some salt and pepper.
5. Grill them for 3 to 5 min on each side. Serve them warm.
6. Enjoy.

ENDIVE
on the Grill

Prep Time: 10 mins
Total Time: 15 mins

Servings per Recipe: 4
Calories   151.0
Fat   7.7 g
Cholesterol   0.0 mg
Sodium   113.9 mg
Carbohydrates   18.0 g
Protein   6.4 g

Ingredients

olive oil
4 Belgian endive halved lengthwise and trimmed
2 tbsp olive oil

1 tbsp oregano, chopped
1 tbsp balsamic vinegar
salt & ground black pepper

Directions

1. Before you do anything, preheat the grill and grease it.
2. Get a large mixing bowl: Toss in it the endive halves with oil, 1/2 tbsp of oregano, a pinch of salt and pepper.
3. Place them on the grill and let them cook for 4 to 5 min on each side.
4. Transfer the grilled endive halves to a serving plate.
5. Drizzle over them some vinegar. Garnish them with some oregano then serve them warm.
6. Enjoy.

Southwest Sirloin

Prep Time: 10 mins
Total Time: 20 mins

Servings per Recipe: 4
Calories	180.1
Fat	5.5 g
Cholesterol	68.0 mg
Sodium	453.9 mg
Carbohydrates	6.6 g
Protein	26.1 g

Ingredients

- 3 tbsp chili powder
- 2 tsp brown sugar
- 2 tsp pepper
- 2 garlic cloves, minced
- 1/2 tsp salt
- 1/2 tsp dried oregano
- 1/4 tsp ground cumin
- 1 lb. boneless beef top sirloin steak
- salsa

Directions

1. Get a mixing bowl: Mix in it the chili powder, brown sugar, pepper, garlic, salt, oregano, and cumin.
2. Massage the mixture into the steak and let it sit for at least 30 min.
3. Before you do anything, preheat the grill and grease it.
4. Grill it for 6 to 8 min on each side. Serve it warm with some salsa.
5. Enjoy.

GERMAN
Pub Food (Topped Smoked Sausage)

🥣 Prep Time: 10 mins
🕐 Total Time: 35 mins

Servings per Recipe: 4
Calories   474.5
Fat   32.6 g
Cholesterol   125.2 mg
Sodium   2742.8 mg
Carbohydrates   23.5 g
Protein   23.3 g

Ingredients

1 1/2 lbs. turkey kielbasa, smoked and halved lengthwise
1 tbsp butter
3 tbsp sugar
1 onion, sliced
3 C. sauerkraut, drained
3 tbsp parsley leaves, chopped

Directions

1. Before you do anything, preheat the grill.
2. Grill the kielbasa for 4 to 6 min on each side.
3. Place a large pan over medium heat. Stir in it the sugar with butter. Heat them until they melt.
4. Stir in it the onions and cook them for 8 to 10 min until they become caramelized.
5. Add the sauerkraut and cook them for 5 to 6 min.
6. Stir in the kielbasa. Cook them for 1 to 2 min.
7. Serve your grilled caramelized kielbasa and onion salad warm.
8. Enjoy.

Grandma's Favorite (Peppery Steak)

Prep Time: 1 hr
Total Time: 1 hr 10 mins

Servings per Recipe: 2
Calories   1379.2
Fat   113.9 g
Cholesterol   308.4 mg
Sodium   598.4 mg
Carbohydrates   3.6 g
Protein   80.2 g

Ingredients

- 1 tsp ground black pepper
- 3/4 tsp chili powder
- 1/4 tsp salt
- 1 1/2 tsp Worcestershire sauce
- 2 tbsp olive oil
- 1 1/2 tsp minced garlic
- 2 tsp minced tarragon
- 2 (16 oz.) bone-in rib eye steaks

Directions

1. Get a mixing bowl: Mix in it the pepper with chili powder, salt, Worcestershire sauce, olive oil, garlic, and tarragon.
2. Massage the mixture into the steaks. Let them sit in the fridge for 60 min.
3. Before you do anything, preheat the grill and grease it.
4. Grill the steaks for 6 to 8 min on each side. Serve them warm.
5. Enjoy.

BLACKENED
Italian Tomatoes

Prep Time: 10 mins
Total Time: 15 mins

Servings per Recipe: 6
Calories   333.5
Fat   29.8 g
Cholesterol   67.6 mg
Sodium   851.8 mg
Carbohydrates   6.0 g
Protein   11.4 g

Ingredients

1 lb. tomatoes, sliced
butter lettuce
1 lb. feta cheese, chunk
2 tbsp extra virgin olive oil
1 bunch basil leaf
1/4 C. extra-virgin olive oil
ground pepper

Directions

1. Before you do anything, preheat the grill and grease it.
2. Arrange the lettuce with tomatoes on a serving plate. Place it aside.
3. Slice the feta into 6 pieces. Brush them with oil and grill them for 1 to 2 min on each side.
4. Arrange them over the tomato slices followed by basil, olive oil, a pinch of salt and pepper.
5. Serve your salad immediately.
6. Enjoy.

Saranac Lake Salmon

Prep Time: 10 mins
Total Time: 15 mins

Servings per Recipe: 4
Calories   513.3
Fat   35.1 g
Cholesterol   135.1 mg
Sodium   272.3 mg
Carbohydrates   0.7 g
Protein   46.8 g

Ingredients

2 lbs. salmon fillets, cut into 4 pieces
1/4 C. vegetable oil
3 tbsp dill, chopped
salt & ground black pepper
4 tbsp melted butter
1/2 lemon, sliced
parsley

Directions

1. Get a mixing bowl: Combine in it the oil with dill, salt, and pepper.
2. Coat the salmon pieces with the mixture. Let them sit for 25 min in the fridge.
3. Before you do anything, preheat the grill and grease it.
4. Drain the salmon pieces and grill them for 4 to 5 min on each side. Serve them warm.
5. Enjoy.

5-INGREDIENT
Salmon

Prep Time: 5 mins
Total Time: 15 mins

Servings per Recipe: 4
Calories   414.4
Fat   29.5 g
Cholesterol   93.5 mg
Sodium   391.2 mg
Carbohydrates   0.1 g
Protein   34.8 g

Ingredients

1/3 C. basil, chopped
2 tbsp olive oil
1/2 tsp salt
1/4 tsp ground pepper

4 (6 oz.) salmon steaks

Directions

1. Before you do anything, preheat the grill and grease it.
2. Get a mixing bowl: Mix in it the basil, olive oil, salt, and pepper.
3. Add the salmon pieces and toss them to coat.
4. Place them on the grill and cook them for 5 to 6 min on each side. Serve them warm.
5. Enjoy.

Grilled Sausage Sandwiches

Prep Time: 25 mins
Total Time: 32 mins

Servings per Recipe: 4
Calories   510.9
Fat   35.2 g
Cholesterol   78.4 mg
Sodium   1832.3 mg
Carbohydrates   30.6 g
Protein   19.1 g

Ingredients

- 1 lb. whole turkey kielbasa, halved lengthwise
- 1/4 C. olive oil
- 2 tbsp Dijon mustard
- 2 tbsp bottled horseradish, drained
- 1 tbsp apple cider vinegar
- 2 1/2 tsp honey
- 1 pinch garlic powder
- 1/4 tsp salt
- ground black pepper
- 1 head Boston lettuce, torn into small pieces
- 2 firm ripe plum tomatoes, sliced
- 4 crusty French rolls

Directions

1. Before you do anything, preheat the grill and grease it.
2. Get a blender: Combine in it the olive oil with mustard, horseradish sauce, vinegar, honey, garlic powder, and salt.
3. Blend them smooth to make the dressing.
4. Get a large mixing bowl: Combine in it the lettuce leaves with half of the dressing. Toss them to coat.
5. Toast the buns on the grill for 1 to 2 min on each side. Grill the kielbasa for 4 to 5 min on each side.
6. Grill the kielbasa pieces for 3 to 4 min on each side.
7. Spread the remaining dressing over the bottom buns.
8. Top them with lettuce, followed by kielbasa pieces, tomatoes, and cheese if you desire.
9. Cover them with the top buns then serve them.
10. Enjoy.

HIBACHI
Sirloin

🍲 Prep Time: 1 min
🕐 Total Time: 5 mins

Servings per Recipe: 4
Calories   236.9
Fat   8.1 g
Cholesterol   85.0 mg
Sodium   1088.1 mg
Carbohydrates   5.7 g
Protein   34.0 g

Ingredients

1 1/4 lbs. boneless beef top sirloin steaks, well-trimmed, cut
Marinade:
3 tbsp soy sauce
2 tsp olive oil
1/2 tsp chili oil
2 tbsp garlic powder, crushed
3/4 tsp pepper
1/3 cilantro, chopped

Sauce
1 tbsp lime juice
1 tbsp soy sauce
1/2 tsp brown sugar, packed
1/4 tsp pepper
Topping
to taste a lime slice
to taste cilantro leaves

Directions

1. Get a mixing bowl:
2. Whisk in it 3 tbsp soy sauce, olive oil and hot chili oil.
3. Get another bowl: Stir in it the garlic powder with 3/4 tsp of pepper.
4. Get a shallow roasting dish: Place in it the beef steaks.
5. Add to it half of the soy mixture with half of the garlic mixture. Stir them to coat.
6. Put on the lid and let them sit for 25 min to marinate.
7. Before you do anything, preheat the grill and grease it.
8. Drain the steak pieces and grill them for 9 to 12 min on each side.
9. Transfer them to a serving plate. Top them with the remaining soy and garlic mixture.
10. Serve them right away.
11. Enjoy.

Nacho for the Summer

Prep Time: 15 mins
Total Time: 30 mins

Servings per Recipe: 4
Calories   1612.3
Fat   129.7 g
Cholesterol   405.8 mg
Sodium   4498.4 mg
Carbohydrates   21.8 g
Protein   88.6 g

Ingredients

- white corn tortilla chips
- 1 lb. zesty hot beef sausage
- 1 lb. ground beef
- 2 (4 oz.) cans mild green chilies
- 1 (1 1/4 oz.) packets taco seasoning
- 2 C. salsa
- 1 bunch green onion, chopped
- 4 C. shredded Mexican blend cheese
- 8 oz. sour cream
- aluminum foil
- cooking spray

Directions

1. Before you do anything, preheat the grill and grease it.
2. Get two large sheets of foil. Coat them with a cooking spray.
3. Divide the nachos between the sheets of foil. Top them with the remaining ingredients.
4. Pull the foil edges over the mixture and pinch it to seal it on top.
5. Grill them for 12 to 16 min on each side. Serve them warm.
6. Enjoy.

DELAWARE
Flat Tortillas

🍲 Prep Time: 10 mins
🕒 Total Time: 20 mins

Servings per Recipe: 4
Calories 556.5
Fat 30.9 g
Cholesterol 59.4 mg
Sodium 1044.6 mg
Carbohydrates 42.1 g
Protein 27.5 g

Ingredients

1 medium cucumber, peeled, seeded and chopped
1/2 C. salsa
8 oz. salmon fillets
3 tbsp olive oil, divided
40 inches flour tortillas, warmed

6 oz. goat cheese, crumbled
1/4 C. pickled jalapeno pepper, drained and sliced

Directions

1. To prepare the salsa:
2. Get a mixing bowl: Stir in it the cucumber and salsa.
3. Place it in the fridge until ready to serve.
4. Before you do anything, preheat the grill and grease it.
5. Coat the salmon pieces with 2 tbsp of olive oil. Season them with a pinch of salt and pepper.
6. Grill them for 6 to 7 min on each side.
7. Heat the tortillas by following the instructions on the package.
8. Place them on a cutting board. Top each one of them with some salmon, cheese, and jalapeno slices.
9. Fold the tortillas and place them aside. Coat them with 1 tbsp of oil.
10. Place a grill pan over medium heat. Toast in it the quesadillas for 2 to 3 min on each side.
11. Serve them warm with the cucumber salsa.
12. Enjoy.

Blackened Chicken Cutlets

Prep Time: 5 mins
Total Time: 13 mins

Servings per Recipe: 4
Calories   154.2
Fat   1.7 g
Cholesterol   68.4 mg
Sodium   1836.4 mg
Carbohydrates   5.3 g
Protein   28.2 g

Ingredients

4 -6 boneless skinless chicken breast halves
Spice Mix
4 tsp granulated onion
4 tsp granulated garlic
1 tbsp kosher salt
2 tsp chili powder
2 tsp ground black pepper
extra virgin olive oil

Directions

1. Before you do anything, preheat the grill and grease it.
2. Get a mixing bowl: Combine in it the onion with garlic, salt, chili powder and black pepper.
3. Coat the chicken dices with the spice mixture. Thread them onto skewers.
4. Grill them for 10 to 14 min. Serve them warm.
5. Enjoy.

GRILLED
Bread

🥣 Prep Time: 15 mins
🕐 Total Time: 21 mins

Servings per Recipe: 4
Calories   112.1
Fat   11.5 g
Cholesterol   30.5 mg
Sodium   84.0 mg
Carbohydrates   2.3 g
Protein   0.6 g

Ingredients

1/4 C. butter
2 tbsp chopped shallots
1/2 tsp chopped garlic
4 slices round sourdough loaf
2 medium Roma tomatoes, cut into 6 slices

1/4 C. torn basil leaf
2 tsp apple cider vinegar

Directions

1. Before you do anything, preheat the grill and grease it.
2. Place a heavy saucepan over medium heat. Heat in it the butter.
3. Cook in it the garlic with shallots for 2 min.
4. Toast the bread slices on the grill for 1 to 2 min on each side.
5. Coat one side of them with butter.
6. Place the buttered side facing down followed by tomato slices and vinegar.
7. Serve them warm.
8. Enjoy.

Maui Night's Dinner (Chicken and Rice)

Prep Time: 25 mins
Total Time: 40 mins

Servings per Recipe: 6
Calories   655.7
Fat   21.9 g
Cholesterol   75.5 mg
Sodium   2822.1 mg
Carbohydrates   78.3 g
Protein   35.5 g

Ingredients

- 6 boneless skinless chicken breasts
- 1 C. soy sauce
- 1 C. pineapple juice
- 1/2 C. vegetable oil
- 2 tbsp brown sugar
- 2 1/2 tsp garlic powder
- 2 tsp ground ginger
- 1 tsp dry mustard
- 1/2 tsp ground pepper
- 6 C. cooked rice
- 6 pineapple rings

Directions

1. Place a heavy saucepan over medium heat: Stir in it the soy sauce, pineapple juice, oil, brown sugar, garlic powder, ginger, dry mustard, and pepper. Heat them until they start boiling. Lower the heat and let them cook for 6 min.
2. Turn off the heat and let the marinade cool down completely.
3. Tenderize the chicken breasts until they become 1/2 inch thick.
4. Get a large zip lock bag: Combine in it the chicken breasts with half of the marinade. Seal the bag and shake it to coat. Place it in the fridge and let it sit overnight.
5. Before you do anything, preheat the grill and grease it.
6. Drain the chicken and breasts and grill them for 6 to 8 min on each side.
7. Coat the pineapple slices with the reserved marinade. Grill them for 3 to 4 min on each side.
8. Serve your tropical chicken breasts and pineapple warm.
9. Enjoy.

LEBANESE
Burgers with White Sauce

🥣 Prep Time: 45 mins
🕐 Total Time: 52 mins

Servings per Recipe: 6
Calories   692.0
Fat   42.4 g
Cholesterol   101.8 mg
Sodium   1017.3 mg
Carbohydrates   46.3 g
Protein   31.2 g

Ingredients

Yogurt Sauce
1 C. plain yogurt
3 tbsp chopped of mint
2 tbsp chopped cilantro
1 1/4 tsp grated lime peel
 kosher salt
Burgers
4 tbsp olive oil, divided
1 1/4 C. chopped onions
2 tbsp minced peeled ginger
2 tsp kosher salt, divided

2 tsp Madras curry powder
1 3/4 lbs. ground lamb
3 tbsp chopped cilantro
1 1/2 tsp cracked black pepper, divided
3 medium zucchini, sliced lengthwise
6 green onions, trimmed
1 poblano chile
6 pita bread
1 large tomatoes, sliced

Directions

1. To prepare the sauce:
2. Get a mixing bowl: Whisk in it the yogurt, mint, cilantro, lime peel, a pinch of salt and pepper.
3. Put on the lid and let it sit in the fridge for 4 h.
4. To prepare the burgers:
5. Place a pan over medium heat. Heat in it 2 tbsp of oil.
6. Cook in it the onion, ginger, and 1/2 tsp. salt for 8 to 9 min.
7. Add the curry powder and cook them for 40 sec.
8. Turn off the heat and let the mixture lose heat for 16 min.
9. Before you do anything, preheat the grill and grease it.
10. Get a mixing bowl: Combine in it the lamb with onion mix, 1 tsp of salt cilantro and 1 tsp of pepper.
11. Mix them well. Shape the mixture into 6 patties.

12. Get a mixing bowl: Toss in it the veggies with 2 tbsp oil, 1/2 tsp. salt, and 1/2 tsp cracked pepper.
13. Grill the burger patties for 5 to 7 min on each side. Grill the veggies for 3 to 4 min on each side.
14. Allow the burgers to rest for 3 to 5 min. Allow the veggies to cool down for a few minutes then chop them.
15. Place the burger patties on the bottom buns. Top them with grilled veggies and raita.
16. Cover them with the top buns then serve them.
17. Enjoy.

FISH
Africano

Prep Time: 15 mins
Total Time: 45 mins

Servings per Recipe: 4
Calories 186.9
Fat 7.6 g
Cholesterol 59.4 mg
Sodium 238.3 mg
Carbohydrates 6.4 g
Protein 24.3 g

Ingredients

1/4 C. nonfat plain yogurt
1/4 C. chopped parsley
1/4 C. chopped cilantro
2 tbsp lemon juice
1 tbsp extra virgin olive oil
3 garlic cloves, minced
1 1/2 tsp paprika
1 tsp ground cumin
1/4 tsp salt
1/8 tsp ground pepper
1 lb. center-cut salmon fillet, cut into 4 portions
1 lemon, cut into wedges

Directions

1. Get a mixing bowl: Whisk in it the yogurt, parsley, cilantro, lemon juice, oil, garlic, paprika, cumin, salt, and pepper.
2. Reserve 1/4 C. of dressing in the fridge until ready to serve.
3. Get a zip lock bag: Combine in it the fish fillets with the remaining dressing.
4. Seal the bag and shake it to coat. Chill it in the fridge to marinade for 35 min.
5. Before you do anything, preheat the grill and grease it.
6. Drain the salmon fillets and grill them for 5 to 7 min on each side.
7. Serve them warm with the reserved dressing sauce.
8. Enjoy.

French Quarter Muffulettas

🥣 Prep Time: 15 mins
🕐 Total Time: 21 mins

Servings per Recipe: 4
Calories   564.4
Fat   49.2 g
Cholesterol   29.2 mg
Sodium   782.0 mg
Carbohydrates   17.9 g
Protein   18.0 g

Ingredients

1 eggplant, sliced
1 zucchini, sliced on an angle
1 red bell pepper, quartered lengthwise
1 large portabella mushroom cap
1 red onion, sliced
1/2 C. extra-virgin olive oil
salt and pepper
6 oz. Baby Spinach

1/3 C. pine nuts
2/3 C. Parmigiano-Reggiano cheese, grated
1 C. giardiniera, store-bought
1/2 C. green olives, pitted
1 (8 -9 inch) round crusty Italian bread
1/4 lb. deli-sliced provolone cheese

Directions

1. To prepare the grilled veggies:
2. Before you do anything, preheat the grill and grease it.
3. Coat the eggplant, zucchini, bell pepper, portobello and red onion with 1/4 C. of olive oil.
4. Sprinkle over them some salt and pepper. Grill them for 3 to 4 min on each side.
5. To prepare the pesto sauce:
6. Get a blender: Combine in it the spinach, pine nuts, Parmigiano-Reggiano, a pinch of salt and pepper.
7. Blend them smooth. Add the rest of the oil gradually while blending.
8. Pour the pesto into a serving bowl. Place it aside.
9. To prepare the relish:
10. Get a food processor: Combine in it the olives with giardiniera. Pulse them several times until they become chopped.
11. Spoon half of the pesto sauce into the bread rolls.
12. Top them with grilled veggies, rest of the pesto sauce and relish. Cover them with the top buns then serve them. Enjoy.

ROSA'S
Taco Tuesdays

Prep Time: 30 mins
Total Time: 1 hr

Servings per Recipe: 6
Calories 148.6
Fat 6.0 g
Cholesterol 76.1 mg
Sodium 155.0 mg
Carbohydrates 1.7 g
Protein 20.9 g

Ingredients

Marinade
2 tbsp diced white onions
2 tbsp olive oil
2 tbsp squeezed lime juice
2 tbsp squeezed orange juice
1 tbsp fresh lemon juice
1 tbsp chopped cilantro
1 tsp minced garlic
1/2 tsp dried oregano, rubbed to a powder
1/4 tsp kosher salt
1 1/2 lbs. boneless skinless white fish fillets

Garnish
corn tortilla, warmed
diced avocados or smashed avocado, with lime juice, and salt
lime wedge
mango salsa
salsa, de chilies de Arbol or bottled hot sauce
pico de gallo

Directions

1. Get a mixing bowl: Whisk in it all the marinade ingredients.
2. Add the fish pieces and stir them to coat. Let it marinate in the fridge for at least 3 h.
3. Before you do anything, preheat the grill and grease it.
4. Drain the fish fillets and grill them for 4 to 6 min on each side.
5. Arrange the avocados on tortillas. Top them with the grilled fish pieces followed by lime juice, mango, and salsa.
6. Wrap your tortillas then serve them.
7. Enjoy.

5-Ingredient Lamb

Prep Time: 10 mins
Total Time: 35 mins

Servings per Recipe: 6
Calories   59.4
Fat   2.6 g
Cholesterol   0.0 mg
Sodium   933.8 mg
Carbohydrates   7.4 g
Protein   3.4 g

Ingredients

- 6 racks of lamb, pat dry
- 2 C. Dijon mustard
- 2 tbsp minced garlic
- 1 tsp oregano
- 1 tsp rosemary

Directions

1. Get a mixing bowl: Mix in it the mustard, garlic, oregano, and rosemary.
2. Coat the lamb racks with the mixture. Let them marinate in the fridge overnight.
3. Before you do anything, preheat the oven to 375 F.
4. Place the lambs on a baking tray. Bake them for 15 min.
5. Once the time is up, remove the tray from the oven and let it cool down for a few minutes.
6. Wrap their tips with a piece of foil.
7. Before you do anything else, preheat the grill and grease it.
8. Grill the racks of lamb for an extra 8 to 12 min on each side.
9. Serve them warm with your favorite sauce.
10. Enjoy.

WEDNESDAY'S
Linguine Dinner

Prep Time: 25 mins
Total Time: 45 mins

Servings per Recipe: 4
Calories   306.7
Fat   5.2 g
Cholesterol   95.5 mg
Sodium   521.4 mg
Carbohydrates   48.8 g
Protein   19.8 g

Ingredients

1 lb. medium shrimp, peeled and deveined
salt
ground black pepper
12 oz. whole wheat linguine
1 tbsp extra virgin olive oil
4 garlic cloves, minced
5 vine-ripened tomatoes, chopped
1/4 C. basil, shredded
1/2 C. brine packed black olives, pitted and chopped
1/2 C. grated low-fat parmesan cheese

Directions

1. Prepare the linguine by following the instructions on the package.
2. Before you do anything else, preheat the grill and grease it.
3. Thread the shrimp onto skewers. Season them with a pinch of salt and pepper.
4. Grill them for 3 to 3 min on each side.
5. Allow the shrimp to cool down for a while then chop each one into 3 pieces.
6. Place a pan over medium heat. Heat in it the oil. Cook in it the garlic for 30 sec.
7. Add the tomato with shrimp and olives. Cook them for 2 to 3 min.
8. Stir in the basil with a pinch of salt and pepper. Spoon your sauce over the linguine.
9. Garnish it with some cheese then serve it.
10. Enjoy.

Chicken
Supremo

Prep Time: 20 mins
Total Time: 50 mins

Servings per Recipe: 4
Calories   639.2
Fat   44.9 g
Cholesterol   160.4 mg
Sodium   10635.5 mg
Carbohydrates   19.3 g
Protein   37.7 g

Ingredients

Marinade
6 tbsp salt
6 tbsp sugar
1/2 tsp pepper, cracked
1 (3 - 3 1/2 lb.) whole chickens
Tapenade
10 pitted Spanish olives

3 tbsp olive oil
1 garlic clove
1 tsp capers

Directions

1. Get a large jug: Combine in it the sugar with water, and salt.
2. Get a large zip lock bag: Place in it the butterflied chicken. Pour over it the water mixture.
3. Seal the bag and let it sit in the fridge for at least 3 h. Drain it and pat it dry.
4. Get a food processor: Combine in it the olives, olive oil, garlic, and capers.
5. Pulse them several times until they become chopped. Massage the mixture into the chicken.
6. Season the chicken with some salt and pepper. Grill it for 15 to 20 min on each side or until it is done.
7. Serve your grilled chicken warm.
8. Enjoy.

HOW TO GRILL
Shiitake Japanese Style

Prep Time: 10 mins
Total Time: 20 mins

Servings per Recipe: 4
Calories 179.4
Fat 16.1 g
Cholesterol 0.0 mg
Sodium 508.5 mg
Carbohydrates 7.6 g
Protein 3.0 g

Ingredients

12 shiitake mushrooms, stemmed
2 tbsp soy sauce
2 tbsp oriental sesame oil
2 tbsp olive oil
4 tsp roasted sesame seeds
2 tsp sugar
1 bunch arugula, stems removed

Directions

1. Get a mixing bowl: Whisk in it the soy sauce, sesame oil, olive oil, and sugar.
2. Before you do anything, preheat the grill and grease it.
3. Arrange the mushroom caps on the grill. Coat them with the soy sauce mixture.
4. Grill them for 3 to 4 min on each side until they become soft.
5. Arrange the arugula on a serving plate.
6. Top it with the remaining soy sauce mixture and grilled mushrooms.
7. Garnish it with sesame seeds then serve it.
8. Enjoy.

Greek
Eggplant Griller

- Prep Time: 20 mins
- Total Time: 28 mins

Servings per Recipe: 6
Calories	238.4
Fat	18.2 g
Cholesterol	37.0 mg
Sodium	469.6 mg
Carbohydrates	13.4 g
Protein	7.9 g

Ingredients

- 2 large aubergines, sliced lengthwise
- 4 tbsp olive oil
- 9 oz. feta cheese
- 1 bunch of mint, chopped
- 1 red chile, chopped
- 1 lemon, juice
- ground black pepper

Directions

1. Before you do anything, preheat the grill and grease it.
2. Coat the aubergine slices with oil. Grill them for 3 to 4 min on each side.
3. Get a mixing bowl: Stir in it the feta cheese and add in the chopped mint, chopped chili, and lemon juice.
4. Season them with a pinch of salt and pepper.
5. Place 1 tsp of feta mixture on the side of one aubergine slice. Roll it tightly and secure it with a toothpick.
6. Repeat the process with the remaining ingredients. Garnish them with some mint and serve them.
7. Enjoy.

FRESH
Herbed Flounder

🥣 Prep Time: 10 mins
🕐 Total Time: 55 mins

Servings per Recipe: 1
Calories   33.9
Fat   0.1 g
Cholesterol   0.0 mg
Sodium   2.3 mg
Carbohydrates   8.3 g
Protein   0.8 g

Ingredients

1 whole flounder, gutted and prepared
1/2 medium orange, sliced
1 tbsp parsley, chopped
1/8 tsp black pepper, ground
1/8 tsp dried basil
1/8 tsp dried oregano
1/8 tsp dried thyme

Directions

1. Before you do anything, preheat the grill and grease it.
2. Get a large piece of foil. Place in it the flounder fish and cover it with the orange slices.
3. Top it with peppers, herbs, a pinch of salt and pepper.
4. Pull the foil over them and pinch it to seal it.
5. Place the fish packet on the grill and let it cook for 35 min.
6. Once the time is up, open the packet and let it cook for another 14 min.
7. Serve it with extra toppings of your choice.
8. Enjoy.

Missouri Style
T-Bone Steaks

Prep Time: 10 mins
Total Time: 25 mins

Servings per Recipe: 4
Calories   364.7
Fat   40.6 g
Cholesterol   0.0 mg
Sodium   178.1 mg
Carbohydrates   1.3 g
Protein   0.2 g

Ingredients

4 beef T-bone steaks
Mustard
3/4 C. extra virgin olive oil
1 1/2 tbsp Dijon mustard
1 tbsp Worcestershire sauce

1/8 tsp kosher salt
1/8 tsp ground black pepper

Directions

1. Before you do anything, preheat the grill and grease it.
2. Get a mixing bowl: Whisk in it the oil with mustard, Worcestershire sauce, salt, and pepper.
3. Coat the steak with the sauce mixture. Grill it for 7 to 9 min on each side.
4. Serve them warm.
5. Enjoy.

FRESH
Herbed 'Matoes

🥣 Prep Time: 10 mins
🕐 Total Time: 20 mins

Servings per Recipe: 12
Calories   55.5
Fat   4.6 g
Cholesterol   0.0 mg
Sodium   8.2 mg
Carbohydrates   3.5 g
Protein   0.7 g

Ingredients

6 green tomatoes, cleaned and sliced
4 tbsp olive oil
1 pinch hot red pepper flakes
1/2 tsp sugar
salt and pepper

2 minced garlic cloves
1 - 2 tsp minced marjoram
1 - 2 tsp minced oregano
3/4 C. grated cheese

Directions

1. Get a large zip lock bag: Place in it the tomato slices, olive oil, Tabasco or hot pepper flakes, sugar, salt and black pepper, garlic, oregano and the marjoram.
2. Season them with a pinch of salt and pepper. Seal the bag and let it sit in the fridge for 8 h.
3. Once the time is up, drain the tomato slices. Put on the lid and let them cook for 3 to 5 min on each side.
4. Garnish them with cheese then serve them warm.
5. Enjoy.

Asian Style Salmon with Basmati Rice

🥣 Prep Time: 45 mins
🕐 Total Time: 1 hr 5 mins

Servings per Recipe: 4
Calories 656.0
Fat 32.0 g
Cholesterol 78.6 mg
Sodium 225.1 mg
Carbohydrates 52.2 g
Protein 41.5 g

Ingredients

Basmati
1 C. basmati rice
1/2 tsp unsalted butter
1 1/2 C. water
2 C. packed the sliced cabbage
1/3 C. packed julienned cucumber
2 tbsp cilantro leaves
2 tbsp mint leaves
Curry Sauce
2 tbsp tomato puree
2 tsp peanut oil
1 tsp minced garlic
1 tsp minced peeled ginger
1 tsp coriander seed, cracked

1 1/2 tsp curry powder
1 1/2 tsp Thai red curry paste
1 1/2 tsp paprika
1/2 tsp ground cumin
1 1/4 C. unsweetened coconut milk
2 tbsp packed brown sugar
2 tsp packed brown sugar
4 (6 oz.) king salmon fillets
1 tbsp olive oil
salt & ground black pepper
1/2 tsp soy sauce
2 tsp rice vinegar
1 tbsp chopped roasted peanuts

Directions

1. For the rice:
2. Prepare the rice by following the instructions on the package.
3. For the salad:
4. Get a mixing bowl: Place in it the cabbage, cucumber, cilantro, and mint. Stir them well.
5. Put on the lid and refrigerate the salad until ready to serve.
6. For the sauce:
7. Place a heavy saucepan over medium heat. Heat in it the peanut oil.
8. Cook in it the garlic with ginger for 2 min.
9. Stir in the coriander seeds, curry powder, curry paste, paprika, and cumin.
10. Lower the heat and let them cook for 2 min.

11. Add the coconut milk, tomato puree, soy sauce, and brown sugar. Cook them for few minutes.
12. Turn off the heat and place the sauce aside.
13. For the fish:
14. Before you do anything, preheat the grill and grease it.
15. Coat the fish fillets with oil. Season them with a pinch of salt and pepper.
16. Grill them for 2 to 3 min on each side. Place them aside to cool down for a while.
17. Add the soy sauce and rice vinegar to the salad. Toss them to coat.
18. Spoon the rice to a serving plate. Pour around them the sauce.
19. Top them with the grilled fish fillets and salad. Serve them immediately.
20. Enjoy.

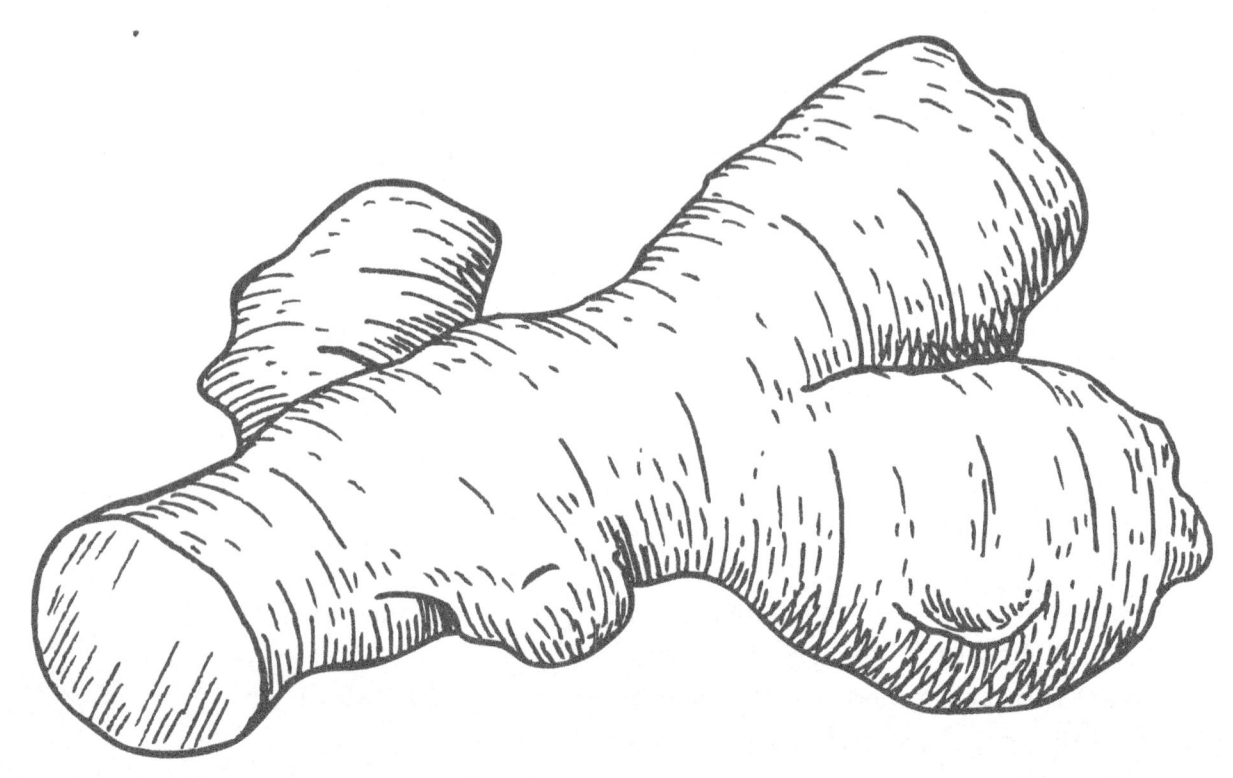

Portuguesa Green Bean Bowls

Prep Time: 15 mins
Total Time: 45 mins

Servings per Recipe: 6
Calories   189.7
Fat   14.8 g
Cholesterol   0.0 mg
Sodium   9.2 mg
Carbohydrates   13.8 g
Protein   2.6 g

Ingredients

- 16 large garlic cloves, unpeeled
- 2 1/2 tbsp extra virgin olive oil
- 1/4 C. extra virgin olive oil
- 1/4 C. balsamic vinegar
- 2 tbsp basil, chopped
- 1 lb. green beans, trimmed
- 1 1/2 C. red onions, sliced
- 3 plum tomatoes, seeded, julienned

Directions

1. Before you do anything, preheat the grill and grease it for 350 F.
2. Get a roasting dish: Combine in it the garlic with 2 tbsp of oil.
3. Put on the lid and let them cook for 22 min in the oven.
4. Once the time is up, remove the cover and let them cook for an extra 9 min. Drain the garlic, peel and add it to blender. Blend them smooth. Pour in the vinegar and blend them smoothly. Pour in 1/4 C. of oil gradually while blending.
5. Pour the mixture into a mixing bowl. Add to it the basil with a pinch of salt and pepper.
6. Bring a large salted pot of water to a boil. Cook in it the beans with a pinch of salt for 2 to 3 min.
7. Drain it and plunge it in an ice bowl of water. Drain it and pat it dry.
8. Get a large mixing bowl: Toss in it the beans with 1/2 tbsp of oil, a pinch of salt and pepper.
9. Before you do anything, preheat the grill and grease it.
10. Place over it the beans and cook them for 1 min on each side.
11. Get a large mixing bowl: Stir in it the beans with onion, tomatoes and garlic dressing.
12. Adjust the seasoning of your salad then serve it.
13. Enjoy.

COOKOUT
Pizzas

🥣 Prep Time: 20 mins
🕐 Total Time: 45 mins

Servings per Recipe: 1
Calories   258.8
Fat   14.4 g
Cholesterol   44.2 mg
Sodium   656.9 mg
Carbohydrates   18.4 g
Protein   15.9 g

Ingredients

- 1 premade 12-inch pizza crust
- 1 -1 1/2 C. spaghetti sauce
- 2 C. mozzarella cheese
- 1 small eggplant, peeled, cut into rounds
- olive oil
- 1/2 C. red bell pepper, chopped
- 2 scallions, chopped
- 1/4 C. red onion, chopped
- 1 C. mushroom, sliced
- 1/2 tsp dried oregano
- 1/2 tsp dried basil
- olive oil
- salt and pepper

Directions

1. Before you do anything, preheat the oven broiler.
2. Get a baking tray. Arrange on top of it the eggplant slices.
3. Pour over it the olive oil. Broil them for 7 to 8 min. Slice each eggplant round in half.
4. Place a skillet over medium heat. Heat in it a drizzle of olive oil.
5. Cook in it the red bell pepper, scallions, red onion, and mushrooms with a pinch of salt for 8 to 12 min.
6. Place the pizza crust on a cookie sheet. Spread over it the spaghetti sauce.
7. Arrange over it the cheese, eggplant, and scallion-red onion-mushroom mixture.
8. Top them with oregano, basil, a drizzle of olive oil, a pinch of salt and pepper.
9. Broil the pizza in the oven for 13 to 15 min. Serve it warm.
10. Enjoy.

California Food Truck Fajitas

🥣 Prep Time: 30 mins
🕒 Total Time: 30 mins

Servings per Recipe: 2
Calories   682.8
Fat   32.2 g
Cholesterol   86.5 mg
Sodium   984.7 mg
Carbohydrates   64.6 g
Protein   32.5 g

Ingredients

1/2 lb. boneless beef top sirloin steak, strips
2 slices onions, separated into rings
1/2 medium green bell pepper, strips
2 tbsp fajita seasoning mix

2 tbsp lime juice
4 (8 inches) flour tortillas
4 tbsp sour cream
4 tbsp chunky salsa

Directions

1. Before you do anything, preheat the grill and grease it.
2. Get a large zip lock bag: Combine in it the steak with onion, bell pepper, and fajita seasoning.
3. Seal the bag and shape it to coat. Arrange the steak and veggies on the grill.
4. Let them cook for 5 to 7 min on each side until they are done to your liking.
5. Get a mixing bowl: Place the steak on a serving plate with the grilled veggies.
6. Pour over them the lime juice and stir them to coat.
7. Arrange steaks strips on tortillas with sour cream.
8. Fold them tightly and toast them on the grill for 1 to 2 min on each side.
9. Serve them warm.
10. Enjoy.

THAI STYLE
Tofu

Prep Time: 10 mins
Total Time: 15 mins

Servings per Recipe: 4
Calories   152.6
Fat   8.3 g
Cholesterol   0.0 mg
Sodium   550.1 mg
Carbohydrates   11.4 g
Protein   10.7 g

Ingredients

1 lb. tofu, cut into triangles
2 tbsp soy sauce
2 tbsp orange juice concentrate
1 tbsp brown sugar
1/4 C. vegetable broth
2 tbsp peanut butter
1/2 tsp brown sugar

1/4 tsp ground ginger
sliced scallion

Directions

1. Get a shallow dish: Whisk in it the soy sauce, orange juice concentrate, and brown sugar.
2. Add the tofu slices and let them sit for 60 min.
3. Before you do anything, preheat the grill and grease it.
4. Drain the tofu slices and grill them for 2 to 3 min on each side.
5. Get a food processor: Combine in it the broth, peanut butter, brown sugar, and ginger. Blend them smooth.
6. Serve your grilled tofu with the peanut sauce. Garnish it with scallions then serve them.
7. Enjoy.

Tuscan Potatoes

Prep Time: 15 hrs
Total Time: 15 hrs 45 mins

Servings per Recipe: 4
Calories   259.3
Fat   7.0 g
Cholesterol   17.9 mg
Sodium   128.0 mg
Carbohydrates   43.3 g
Protein   6.3 g

Ingredients

6 small red potatoes, unpeeled, chopped
1 C. baby carrots, halved lengthwise
2 tbsp butter, melted
1/2 tsp dried Italian seasoning
1/2 tsp peppered seasoning salt

2 tbsp shredded parmesan cheese
2 tbsp chopped chives

Directions

1. Before you do anything, preheat the grill and grease it.
2. Get a large piece of foil. Combine in it the carrots with potatoes.
3. Pour over it the melted butter with Italian seasoning, peppered seasoning salt, and cheese.
4. Stir them to coat. Pull the edges of the foil over the mixture and pinch it to seal.
5. Place it over the grill and let it cook for 46 to 52 min. Serve it warm.
6. Enjoy.

PASTA SALAD
Penne

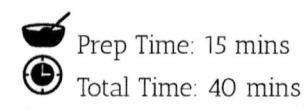

Prep Time: 15 mins
Total Time: 40 mins

Servings per Recipe: 4
Calories   1066.0
Fat   67.0 g
Cholesterol   125.6 mg
Sodium   417.1 mg
Carbohydrates   71.1 g
Protein   47.0 g

Ingredients

1/3 C. capers
1/2 C. unsalted butter
1 1/2 lbs. tuna, cut into chunks
2 tbsp vegetable oil
salt
 cracked black pepper
12 oz. penne

1/2 C. olive oil
1/4 C. lemon juice
2 tbsp minced garlic
1/2 C. chopped parsley

Directions

1. Before you do anything, place a heavy saucepan over medium heat.
2. Stir in it the butter with capers. Cook them until they start simmering.
3. Let them cook for 8 to 10 min. Strain the capers and place them aside.
4. Thread the tuna chunks onto skewers. Coat them with oil. Season them with a pinch of salt and pepper.
5. Grill the tuna skewers for 4 to 5 min on each side.
6. Prepare the pasta by following the instructions on the package.
7. Get a large mixing bowl: Stir in it the noodles with capers, olive oil, lemon juice, garlic, parsley, grilled tuna and salt and pepper.
8. Adjust the seasoning of your spaghetti then serve it warm.
9. Enjoy.

Pittsburgh Dijon Trout

Prep Time: 10 mins
Total Time: 22 mins

Servings per Recipe: 4
Calories   135.4
Fat   5.4 g
Cholesterol   45.8 mg
Sodium   124.8 mg
Carbohydrates   4.0 g
Protein   16.6 g

Ingredients

4 rainbow trout fillets
2 tbsp thawed apple juice concentrate
1 tbsp Dijon mustard
1 tsp cider vinegar
1/2 tsp paprika

1/4 tsp pepper
1 pinch salt

Directions

1. Before you do anything, preheat the grill and grease it.
2. Get a mixing bowl: Whisk in it the apple juice concentrate, mustard, vinegar, paprika, pepper, and salt.
3. Massage the mixture into the fish fillets. Grill them for 5 to 7 min on each side. Serve them warm.
4. Enjoy..

BLACKENED Grapes

Prep Time: 1 min
Total Time: 5 mins

Servings per Recipe: 1
Calories	106.8
Fat	2.4 g
Cholesterol	0.0 mg
Sodium	2.5 mg
Carbohydrates	22.8 g
Protein	0.9 g

Ingredients

1 small cluster red seedless grapes
1/2 tsp olive oil

Directions

1. Before you do anything, preheat the grill and grease it.
2. Coat the cluster of grapes with olive oil. Grill them for 1 to 2 min on each side.
3. Serve your grilled grapes warm or cold.
4. Enjoy.

Grilled Garlic Bread

Prep Time: 5 mins
Total Time: 10 mins

Servings per Recipe: 6
Calories   93.2
Fat   3.2 g
Cholesterol   2.7 mg
Sodium   221.6 mg
Carbohydrates   12.6 g
Protein   3.3 g

Ingredients

1/3 C. pitted black olives, sliced
3 tbsp parmesan cheese, grated
1/2 small red onion, chopped
1/2 tsp garlic, crushed

1/2 tsp vegetable stock powder
1 large French breadstick

Directions

1. Before you do anything, preheat the oven broiler.
2. Get a food processor: Combine in it the olives with cheese, onion, garlic and stock powder.
3. Blend them smooth.
4. Slice the breadstick into the round. Coat one side of each bread slice with the cheese mixture.
5. Arrange them on a baking tray. Grill them for 2 to 3 min. Serve them warm.
6. Enjoy.

MEGAN'S
Garden Polenta

🥣 Prep Time: 15 mins
🕐 Total Time: 55 mins

Servings per Recipe: 4
Calories	208.1
Fat	8.0 g
Cholesterol	0.0 mg
Sodium	28.1 mg
Carbohydrates	31.8 g
Protein	4.4 g

Ingredients

3 C. water
1 tbsp dried Italian herb seasoning
1 C. cornmeal
1 tbsp balsamic vinegar
2 garlic cloves, minced
1 tbsp brown sugar
1/2 lb. asparagus spear

1/2 lb. tomatoes, sliced
2 tbsp olive oil
Topping
parsley
shaved parmesan cheese
salt and pepper

Directions

1. Place a large saucepan over high heat. Heat in it 2 C. of water until they start boiling. Add the herbs with polenta, a pinch of salt and pepper. Lower the heat and let them cook while stirring until they become thick. Cover a baking dish with a piece of foil.
2. Pour in it the polenta mixture and spread it into an even layer.
3. Let it lose heat for 8 h.
4. Before you do anything, preheat the grill and grease it.
5. Once the time is up, slice the polenta block into shapes of your choice. Coat them with oil then sprinkle over them some salt and pepper. Place the polenta pieces on the grill. Let them cook for 1 to 2 min on each side. Place a heavy saucepan over medium heat. Combine in it the balsamic vinegar, garlic, and sugar.
6. Stir them until the sugar dissolves. Add the asparagus and let them cook for 3 to 4 min. Place your grilled polenta on a serving plate.
7. Arrange over it the saucy asparagus with tomato, cheese, and parsley. Drizzle over them some olive oil. Serve it right away.
8. Enjoy.

Squash over Pasta

Prep Time: 10 mins
Total Time: 30 mins

Servings per Recipe: 2
Calories 356.0
Fat 9.8 g
Cholesterol 4.4 mg
Sodium 100.1 mg
Carbohydrates 56.0 g
Protein 12.9 g

Ingredients

- 4 oz. uncooked angel hair pasta
- 1 1/2 tbsp lemon juice
- 1 tbsp olive oil
- 2 cloves garlic, minced
- 1 tbsp dried basil
- 2 small yellow squash, halved lengthwise
- 3 medium tomatoes, halved
- salt
- 1/4 tsp ground black pepper
- 2 tbsp parmesan cheese, grated

Directions

1. Prepare the pasta by following the instructions on the package.
2. Get a mixing bowl: Mix in it the squash, tomatoes, oil, garlic, salt, basil, and pepper.
3. Before you do anything, preheat the grill and grease it.
4. Arrange on it the veggies and let them cook for 4 to 6 min on each side.
5. Chop them into small pieces.
6. Get a large mixing bowl: Toss in it the grilled veggies with pasta, a pinch of salt and pepper.
7. Garnish it with cheese then serve it warm.
8. Enjoy.

GRITS
in the Summer

Prep Time: 15 mins
Total Time: 1 hr 5 mins

Servings per Recipe: 8
Calories   144.8
Fat   6.7 g
Cholesterol   14.9 mg
Sodium   382.7 mg
Carbohydrates   15.7 g
Protein   5.0 g

Ingredients

4 C. water
1 C. uncooked old fashion grits
1 tsp salt
4 oz. shredded cheddar cheese

1 - 2 clove garlic, minced
1 tbsp olive oil

Directions

1. Place a large saucepan over medium heat. Heat in it the water until it starts boiling.
2. Add the grits with salt. Cook them while stirring until they start simmering.
3. Lower the heat and let it cook for 42 to 46 min while stirring it often.
4. Once the time is up, stir in the garlic with cheese.
5. Grease a baking dish with some oil. Pour in it the grits and put on the lid.
6. Let it cool down for a while. Chill it in the fridge for 120 to 200 min.
7. Before you do anything, preheat the grill and grease it.
8. Slice the grits block into 3 inches square.
9. Coat it them with oil and grill them for 5 to 7 min on each side. Serve them warm. Enjoy.

Persian Style Lamb Chops

🥣 Prep Time: 15 mins
🕐 Total Time: 25 mins

Servings per Recipe: 2
Calories   336.3
Fat   36.0 g
Cholesterol   0.0 mg
Sodium   3.1 mg
Carbohydrates   4.1 g
Protein   0.7 g

Ingredients

2 small racks of lamb
salt & ground black pepper
1 sprig rosemary leaf
1/4 C. pomegranate juice

5 cloves garlic, crushed
1 shallot, diced
1/3 C. virgin olive oil

Directions

1. Rub the rosemary leaves with a pinch of salt and pepper into the lamb chops.
2. Get a large zip lock bag: Combine in it the molasses, garlic, shallot, and oil.
3. Place in it the lamb chops and seal it. Shake it to coat. Let it sit in the fridge for 5 h.
4. Before you do anything, preheat the grill and grease it.
5. Drain the lamb chops and cook them for 6 to 8 min on each side.
6. Serve them warm with toppings of your choice.
7. Enjoy.

SPANISH
Millet Salad

Prep Time: 10 mins
Total Time: 40 mins

Servings per Recipe: 4
Calories   496.4
Fat   24.9 g
Cholesterol   0.0 mg
Sodium   31.7 mg
Carbohydrates   67.8 g
Protein   9.1 g

Ingredients

1 C. millet
20 oz. unsalted vegetable stock
1 red pepper
1 yellow pepper
1 orange bell pepper
6 tbsp extra virgin olive oil
1 onion, chopped
2 garlic cloves, chopped
1 red chili, deseeded and chopped
1 tsp ground mixed spice
2 ripe tomatoes, skinned and diced
2 tbsp balsamic vinegar
2 tbsp chopped basil
salt & ground black pepper

Directions

1. Place a large skillet over medium heat. Toast in it the millet for 4 min while stirring. Transfer it to a saucepan. Stir in the stock with a pinch of salt. Cook them until they start boiling.
2. Lower the heat and let them cook for 22 to 26 min while stirring often. Before you do anything, preheat the grill and grease it.
3. Grill the peppers for 6 to 8 min on each side. Place them aside to cool down for a while.
4. Peel them, cored them, seed them and cut them into strips.
5. Place a skillet over medium heat. Heat in it 1 tbsp of oil.
6. Cook in it the onion, garlic, chili and mixed spice. Cook them for 4 to 5 min.
7. Stir in the tomatoes and heat them for 2 to 3 min.
8. Stir the rest of the oil with vinegar, a pinch of salt and pepper into the millet.
9. Add the tomato mix with basil and pepper strips. Mix them well.
10. Adjust the seasoning of your millet then serve it warm.
11. Enjoy.

Milanese Tomatoes

Prep Time: 10 mins
Total Time: 25 mins

Servings per Recipe: 4
Calories   26.1
Fat   0.2 g
Cholesterol   0.0 mg
Sodium   152.8 mg
Carbohydrates   5.7 g
Protein   1.2 g

Ingredients

- 2 garlic cloves, minced
- 2 tbsp Italian parsley, chopped
- 1 tsp lemon rind, grated
- 1 tbsp fresh lemon juice
- 1/4 tsp sea salt
- 1 pinch pepper
- 4 tomatoes, halved

Directions

1. Before you do anything, preheat the grill and grease it.
2. Get a mixing bowl: Mix in it the garlic with parsley, lemon rind, and juice, a pinch of salt and pepper.
3. Arrange the tomato halves with the cut upside facing up on the grill.
4. Spoon over them the parsley sauce.
5. Let them cook for 10 to 14 min until they become soft then serve them warm.
6. Enjoy.

GRILLED Fruit Bowls

🥣 Prep Time: 15 mins
🕒 Total Time: 18 mins

Servings per Recipe: 4
Calories   149.4
Fat   7.3 g
Cholesterol   0.0 mg
Sodium   0.7 mg
Carbohydrates   22.0 g
Protein   1.9 g

Ingredients

6 plums, halved and pitted
2 tsp canola oil
1 tbsp honey
1 pinch ground cinnamon
1 pinch grated orange zest
Yogurt Sauce
1 C. Greek yogurt
1 tbsp honey
2 tbsp orange juice

1 tsp grated orange zest
1/4 tsp ground cinnamon
1/4 C. chopped walnuts, toasted

Directions

1. Get a mixing bowl: Whisk in it all the yogurt sauce ingredients.
2. Place it in the fridge until ready to serve.
3. Before you do anything preheat the grill and grease it.
4. Coat the cut upside of the plums with oil.
5. Drizzle over them honey with a pinch of orange zest and cinnamon.
6. Place them on the grill with the oily side facing down. Let them cook for 2 to 3 min.
7. Flip the plums and let them cook for another minute on the other side.
8. Place your plums on serving plates. Top them with yogurt sauce.
9. Chill them in the fridge until ready to serve.
10. Enjoy.

Lighthouse Steaks

Prep Time: 12 hrs
Total Time: 12 hrs 10 mins

Servings per Recipe: 3
Calories	496.4
Fat	27.9 g
Cholesterol	92.9 mg
Sodium	2915.1 mg
Carbohydrates	6.6 g
Protein	53.3 g

Ingredients

- 1 lemon, juice
- 1/2 C. soy sauce
- 1/4 C. apple cider vinegar
- 2 tbsp vegetable oil
- 2 tbsp Worcestershire sauce
- 1 large garlic clove, sliced
- pepper
- green onion, chopped
- dill weed, chopped
- celery seed
- 1 1/2 lbs. flank steaks, trimmed

Directions

1. Get a large zip lock bag: Place in it the steaks.
2. Pour over them the remaining ingredients then seal the bag. Shake it to coat.
3. Place it in the fridge and let it sit for 3 to 14 h in the fridge.
4. Before you do anything, preheat the grill and grease it.
5. Drain the steaks and cook them for 7 to 10 min on each side. Serve them warm.
6. Enjoy.

GREEK STYLE
Potatoes

🥣 Prep Time: 10 mins
🕐 Total Time: 40 mins

Servings per Recipe: 8
Calories   237.2
Fat   6.9 g
Cholesterol   0.0 mg
Sodium   451.3 mg
Carbohydrates   40.3 g
Protein   4.7 g

Ingredients

4 lbs. small red potatoes, halved
1/4 C. olive oil, divided
1 tbsp grated lemon juice
2 garlic cloves, pressed
1 1/2 tsp salt
1/2 tsp ground pepper
1/3 C. parsley, chopped
vegetable oil cooking spray

Directions

1. Place a large salted pot of water to a boil.
2. Add to it the potatoes and cook them for 22 to 26 min until they become soft.
3. Once the time is up, drain them and transfer them to a mixing bowl.
4. Add to them 2 tbsp of oil with a pinch of salt and pepper.
5. Before you do anything else, preheat the grill and grease it.
6. Arrange the potatoes on the grill and cook them for 6 min while flipping them.
7. Get a shallow dish: Combine in it the remaining oil with lemon juice, garlic, parsley, a pinch of salt and pepper.
8. Add the grilled potatoes then toss them to coat. Serve it warm.
9. Enjoy.

Garden Turkey Cutlets

Prep Time: 10 mimns
Total Time: 1 hr 40 mins

Servings per Recipe: 8
Calories   292.2
Fat   14.4 g
Cholesterol   103.4 mg
Sodium   261.7 mg
Carbohydrates   8.3 g
Protein   31.7 g

Ingredients

- 1 turkey breast
- 1/4 C. parsley sprig
- 1/4 C. basil leaf
- 3 tbsp butter
- 4 garlic cloves, halved
- 1/2 tsp salt
- 1 medium lemon, sliced
- 1 medium orange, sliced
- 1 tbsp cornstarch
- 2 tbsp water
- 1 C. orange juice
- 1 tsp orange peel, grated
- 1 tsp lemon peel, grated
- 1/4 tsp pepper

Directions

1. Before you do anything, preheat the grill using indirect heat and grease it. Get a blender: Place in it the parsley, basil, butter, garlic, and salt. Blend them smooth.
2. Massage the mixture into the chicken while reaching under the skin. Slide the orange and lemon slices between the meat and turkey breast. Secure them with toothpicks.
3. Grill the turkey breast for 2 h to 2 h 20 min while turning it every once in a while.
4. Wrap a piece of foil around the turkey breast and let it rest for 12 min.
5. Place a heavy saucepan over medium heat. Combine in it the water with cornstarch.
6. Add the orange juice, orange peel, lemon peel, pepper, and salt.
7. Cook them while stirring until they start boiling.
8. Lower the heat and let them cook for 2 to 3 min until the sauce becomes thick.
9. Spoon the sauce over the turkey breast then serve it warm.
10. Enjoy.

TROPICAL
Skewers

Prep Time: 1 hr
Total Time: 1 hr 30 mins

Servings per Recipe: 3
Calories 559.9
Fat 28.3 g
Cholesterol 193.7 mg
Sodium 199.7 mg
Carbohydrates 7.6 g
Protein 66.8 g

Ingredients

2 lbs. chicken breasts, diced
2 C. Lawry teriyaki marinade with pineapple juice
whole pineapple, sliced

16 oz. baby portabella mushrooms

Directions

1. Get a mixing bowl: Stir in it all the ingredients.
2. Cover it and let it sit in the fridge for at least 1 h.
3. Before you do anything, preheat the grill and grease it.
4. Drain the chicken, pineapple, and mushrooms from the marinade.
5. Thread them onto skewers and grill them for 5 to 6 min on each side.
6. Serve them warm.
7. Enjoy.

Grilled Caprese Ciabatta

Prep Time: 20 mimns
Total Time: 20 mins

Servings per Recipe: 6
Calories	14.7
Fat	0.1 g
Cholesterol	0.0 mg
Sodium	4.1 mg
Carbohydrates	3.1 g
Protein	0.7 g

Ingredients

- 12 -16 slices ciabatta
- 2 - 3 garlic cloves
- 4 medium tomatoes, ripe
- extra virgin olive oil
- salt

Directions

1. Before you do anything, preheat the grill and grease it.
2. Grill your ciabatta slices for 1 to 2 min on a side.
3. Cut the cloves of garlic in half and rub the ciabatta slices with them.
4. Repeat the process with the tomato. Brush them with oil then season them with a pinch of salt.
5. Serve them right away.
6. Enjoy.

TROUT 101

🥣 Prep Time: 5 mins
🕐 Total Time: 17 mins

Servings per Recipe: 4
Calories   482.5
Fat   31.2 g
Cholesterol   145.5 mg
Sodium   276.6 mg
Carbohydrates   6.1 g
Protein   43.6 g

Ingredients

4 (7 oz.) whole trout
vegetable oil
salt and pepper
2 oz. butter
2 oz. cashew nuts, shelled

2 garlic cloves, chopped
chopped parsley
1 lemon, juice

Directions

1. Before you do anything, preheat the grill and grease it.
2. Cut 3 slits in the trout. Coat it with oil then season it with a pinch of salt and pepper.
3. Grill it for 4 to 6 min on each side.
4. Place a large skillet over medium heat. Heat in it the butter until it melts.
5. Place in it the grilled trout and fry it for 1 to 2 min on each side.
6. Drain it and transfer it to a serving plate.
7. Stir the garlic with parsley into the same skillet. Cook it for 40 sec to 1 min.
8. Stir in the lemon juice with a pinch of salt and pepper. Heat them for few seconds.
9. Drizzle the sauce over the grilled trout then serve it right away.
10. Enjoy.

How to Grill Collard Greens

Prep Time: 10 mins
Total Time: 25 mins

Servings per Recipe: 8
Calories   37.0
Fat   0.5 g
Cholesterol   0.0 mg
Sodium   894.8 mg
Carbohydrates   7.0 g
Protein   3.0 g

Ingredients

2 bunches collard greens, trimmed and washed
1 tbsp salt
2 tbsp bacon fat, optional

ice water
salt & ground black pepper

Directions

1. Before you do anything, preheat the grill and grease it.
2. Place a large pot of water over high heat. Stir in it the fat with a pinch of salt.
3. Heat in it until it starts boiling. Stir in the greens and cook them for 3 to 4 min.
4. Drain them and place it in an ice cold bowl of water. Drain them and pat them dry.
5. Coat your greens with oil then grill for 4 to 5 min on each side until they become crunchy.
6. Serve them right away with a dipping sauce of your choice.
7. Enjoy.

SIMPLE Salmon

Prep Time: 5 mins
Total Time: 17 mins

Servings per Recipe: 4
Calories   276.5
Fat   21.0 g
Cholesterol   59.0 mg
Sodium   60.9 mg
Carbohydrates   1.1 g
Protein   20.0 g

Ingredients

4 salmon steaks
3 tbsp olive oil
2 tbsp lemon juice
1 spring onion, minced
6 tbsp limoncello
1 tsp oregano
2 tbsp minced parsley

Directions

1. Get a large mixing bowl: Whisk in it the olive oil, lemon, onion, liqueur, oregano and salt and ground pepper.
2. Add the salmon steaks and coat them with the marinade. Cover them and let them sit in the fridge for 4 to 7 h.
3. Before you do anything, preheat the grill and grease it.
4. Drain the steaks and grill them for 6 to 8 min on each side. Serve them warm.
5. Enjoy.

House Special Couscous

Prep Time: 5 mins
Total Time: 20 mins

Servings per Recipe: 2
Calories	662.5
Fat	29.4 g
Cholesterol	0.0 mg
Sodium	608.9 mg
Carbohydrates	82.7 g
Protein	18.8 g

Ingredients

- 2 large tomatoes, cored and quartered
- 4 tbsp olive oil
- 10 broccoli florets
- 6 oz. green beans, trimmed
- 175 g couscous
- 1/2 tsp cinnamon
- 1/2 tsp cumin
- 1/2 tsp ground coriander
- 1/2 tsp chili powder
- 1 1/2 C. hot chicken stock
- 1/2 lemon, juice
- 7 oz. halloumi cheese, cut into 4 to 6 slices
- salt and pepper

Directions

1. Before you do anything, preheat the oven to 350 F.
2. Coat the tomatoes with oil. Sprinkle over them some salt and pepper.
3. Arrange on a cookie sheet. Cook them in the oven for 12 to 16 min.
4. Prepare a steamer. Steam in it the beans with broccoli for 7 min.
5. Get a large mixing bowl: Stir in it the couscous with stock, and spices.
6. Put on the lid and let them sit for 6 min. Fluff them with a fork.
7. Add the lemon juice with beans and broccoli. Mix them well.
8. Serve your broiled tomatoes with couscous salad with halloumi cheese.
9. Enjoy.

INDEPENDENCE
Catfish

🥣 Prep Time: 10 mins
🕐 Total Time: 20 mins

Servings per Recipe: 8
Calories   221.2
Fat   12.2 g
Cholesterol   74.7 mg
Sodium   375.6 mg
Carbohydrates   1.3 g
Protein   25.0 g

Ingredients

1 tbsp paprika
1 tsp salt
2 tsp thyme
2 tsp oregano
2 tsp garlic powder

1 tsp ground black pepper
1 tsp ground red pepper
8 catfish fillets

Directions

1. Before you do anything, preheat the grill and grease it.
2. Get a mixing bowl: Mix in it all the spices. Rub them into the fish fillets.
3. Pace them on the grill and cook them for 4 to 6 min on each side. Serve them right away.
4. Enjoy.

Chicken
Salad Summers

 Prep Time: 20 mins
 Total Time: 35 mins

Servings per Recipe: 3
Calories   319.0
Fat   7.9 g
Cholesterol   189.9 mg
Sodium   392.5 mg
Carbohydrates   31.5 g
Protein   31.4 g

Ingredients

- 1/2 lb. boneless skinless chicken breast
- 2 tbsp lemon juice
- 1 tsp olive oil
- 1 tsp lemon pepper
- 1/2 tsp garlic powder
- 1/4 C. plain fat-free yogurt
- 2 tbsp honey
- 2 tbsp Dijon mustard
- 1 tsp sugar
- 1/8 tsp garlic powder
- 6 C. lettuce, torn
- 1 tomatoes, large cut into 8 wedges
- 1 C. cucumber, sliced
- 1 C. cooked potato, diced
- 2 eggs, hard boiled and diced
- 1/2 C. radish, sliced
- 1/2 C. cheddar cheese, shredded

Directions

1. Get a large zip lock bag: Place in the chicken breasts.
2. Get a mixing bowl: Whisk in it the lemon juice, olive oil, lemon pepper, and 1/2 t. garlic powder. Pour the marinade over the chicken and seal the bag. Shake it to coat.
3. Place it in the fridge and let it sit for at least 40 min.
4. Get a mixing bowl: Whisk in it the yogurt, honey, mustard, sugar and 1/8 tsp garlic powder to make the sauce.
5. Place it in the fridge until ready to serve.
6. Before you do anything, preheat the grill and grease it.
7. Drain the chicken breasts from the marinade and cook them for 4 to 6 min on each side. Wrap them in a piece of foil and let them rest for 12 min.
8. Once the time is up, transfer the chicken breasts between serving plates. Top them with the yogurt sauce, lettuce, tomato, cucumber, potato, eggs, radish and cheese on top.
9. Serve them right away.
10. Enjoy.

GRAPEFRUIT
Griller

🥣 Prep Time: 10 mins
⏱ Total Time: 15 mins

Servings per Recipe: 2
Calories   115.6
Fat   0.1 g
Cholesterol   0.0 mg
Sodium   0.8 mg
Carbohydrates   30.4 g
Protein   1.0 g

Ingredients

1 pink grapefruit, peeled and quartered
2 tbsp honey
1 pinch ground allspice
mint sprig

Directions

1. Before you do anything, preheat the grill and grease it.
2. Place the grapefruit quarters in a shallow roasting pan.
3. Get a mixing bowl: Whisk in it the honey with allspice. Drizzle them over the grapefruit.
4. Place the pan directly over the grill heat. Let them cook for 6 min.
5. Serve your grilled grapefruit warm with some ice cream.
6. Enjoy.

Park Ave
Fig Kabobs

Prep Time: 10 mins
Total Time: 14 mins

Servings per Recipe: 4
Calories   112.7
Fat   0.1 g
Cholesterol   0.0 mg
Sodium   1.5 mg
Carbohydrates   30.0 g
Protein   0.5 g

Ingredients

4 stalks rosemary
4 large firm ripe figs, stems trimmed, halved lengthwise
1/4 C. liquid honey
1 tbsp lemon juice, squeezed
ground black pepper

Directions

1. Pull the rosemary leaves from the stalk leaving the only ones on top.
2. Measure 2 tbsp of rosemary leaves and chop them.
3. Get a bowl: Place in it the rosemary stems and cover them with water.
4. Let them sit for 35 min. Drain them and dry them.
5. Before you do anything, preheat the grill and grease it.
6. Thread each two fig halves onto 2 rosemary stems.
7. Get a mixing bowl: Whisk in it the honey with lemon juice. Coat the figs skewers with it.
8. Grill them for 2 to 3 min on each side. Serve them hot with some ice cream.
9. Enjoy.

HOW TO
Grill Oysters

🥣 Prep Time: 20 mins
🕐 Total Time: 22 mins

Servings per Recipe: 4
Calories	289.3
Fat	7.4 g
Cholesterol	150.4 mg
Sodium	577.6 mg
Carbohydrates	24.5 g
Protein	29.2 g

Ingredients

1 small onion, grated
1/4 C. hoisin sauce
3 cloves garlic, minced
1/2 tsp hot pepper flakes
24 large raw shucked oysters, patted dry
2 tbsp cilantro, chopped
12 wooden skewers, soaked

Directions

1. Get a mixing bowl: Mix in it the onion with hoisin sauce, garlic, and pepper flakes.
2. Stir in the oysters. Put on the lid and let them sit for 16 min.
3. Before you do anything, preheat the grill and grease it.
4. Drain the oysters and thread them onto skewers.
5. Grill them for 1 to 2 min on each side with basting them with the marinade.
6. Serve them hot right away.
7. Enjoy.

Texan Steak Toppers

Prep Time: 30 mins
Total Time: 1 hr 10 mins

Servings per Recipe: 4
Calories   589.2
Fat   31.1 g
Cholesterol   34.5 mg
Sodium   1053.9 mg
Carbohydrates   66.7 g
Protein   12.2 g

Ingredients

- 16 round butter-flavored crackers
- 16 fresh spinach leaves
- 1/3 C. blue cheese, crumbles
- sea salt
- cracked black pepper
- sriracha sauce
- Potatoes
- 2 red potatoes, unpeeled, diced
- 2 slices turkey bacon, cooked and crumbled
- 1 tbsp Hidden Valley Original Ranch Dips Mix
- 1 tbsp snipped fresh chives
- 2 tbsp Greek yogurt
- 1 tsp grated garlic
- Onion rings
- 2 large shallots, peeled and sliced into 6-8 rings each
- 1 - 2 tbsp melted butter
- 1/3 C. seasoned dry breadcrumb
- 1 tsp grated parmesan cheese
- Steak
- 1 thick-cut ribeye steak
- 1 tbsp Hidden Valley Original Ranch Dips Mix
- 2 tbsp melted butter

Directions

1. To prepare the potatoes:
2. Place a large saucepan over high heat. Place in it the potatoes with a pinch of salt.
3. Cover them with water and bring them to a boil. Let them cook for 16 to 22 min until they become soft.
4. Drain the potatoes and transfer them to a blender. Add the garlic with ranch sauce, chives, and yogurt.
5. Blend them smooth. Pour the mixture into a bowl. Stir into it the bacon and put on the lid.
6. Place it in the fridge and let it sit until ready to serve.
7. To prepare the onion rings:
8. Before you do anything, preheat the oven to 375 F.

9. Get a mixing bowl: Stir in it the shallot rings with melted butter, parmesan cheese and breadcrumbs.
10. Spread the mixture on a lined up baking sheet. Bake them for 16 to 22 min.
11. To prepare the steak:
12. Before you do anything, preheat the grill and grease it.
13. Season the steaks with a pinch of salt and pepper.
14. Massage the ranch dip into the steak then coat it with melted butter.
15. Grill it for 6 to 8 min on each side. Let it rest for 6 min then slice it.
16. Arrange the crackers on a serving platter.
17. Top them with warm mashed potatoes, spinach leaves, slices of steak, shallot rings, and blue cheese crumbles.
18. Serve them right away.
19. Enjoy.

African Lamb with Chili Sauce

Prep Time: 1 hr 24 mins
Total Time: 1 hr 54 mins

Servings per Recipe: 2
Calories 832.6
Fat 67.1 g
Cholesterol 179.6 mg
Sodium 206.0 mg
Carbohydrates 13.5 g
Protein 43.6 g

Ingredients

Marinade
1 tbsp coriander seeds, ground
1 tbsp cumin seed, ground
3 tbsp harissa
1 lemon, juice
2 tbsp extra-virgin olive oil
4 garlic cloves, minced
Lamb
1 - 3 lb. lamb shoulder, boned and butterflied
kosher salt & ground black pepper
Yogurt Sauce
1 C. yogurt
1 C. cucumber, peeled, seeded and grated
1/4 C. mint, minced
3 tbsp preserved lemons, minced
kosher salt & ground black pepper

Directions

1. To prepare the marinade:
2. Get a mixing bowl: Mix in it the ground coriander seeds with cumin, harissa, lemon juice, olive oil, garlic, and coriander.
3. Sprinkle some salt and pepper all over the lamb shoulder. Coat it with the oil mixture. Place it in a large zip lock bag and seal it. Let it sit in the fridge for 2 h. Get a mixing bowl: Mix in it the yogurt, cucumber, mint, preserved lemon, a pinch of salt and pepper.
4. Place it in the fridge until ready to serve.
5. Before you do anything else, preheat the grill and grease it.
6. Slice the lamb shoulder into pieces. Grill them for 6 to 8 min on each side. Before you do anything, preheat the oven to 350 min.
7. Arrange the lamb pieces on a baking tray. Layover them a piece of foil and bake them for 20 to 35 min. Serve them warm with the yogurt salsa. Enjoy.

MICHELLE'S
Tilapia

Prep Time: 30 mins
Total Time: 1 hr 15 mins

Servings per Recipe: 4
Calories	290.1
Fat	9.6 g
Cholesterol	92.6 mg
Sodium	453.0 mg
Carbohydrates	14.9 g
Protein	37.5 g

Ingredients

Reynolds Wrap Foil
4 large unfrozen tilapia fillets
8 slices Applewood smoked turkey bacon
1 dash pepper
1 dash garlic powder
1 lime, juice
2 large yellow peaches, diced
1 small sweet onion, minced
1 small red bell pepper, minced
1 tsp honey
salt and pepper
1 bunch cilantro

Directions

1. To prepare the salsa:
2. Get a mixing bowl: Combine in it the peaches with minced pepper, onion, lime juice, honey, cilantro and a pinch of salt.
3. Place it in the fridge until ready to serve.
4. To prepare the fish:
5. Before you do anything, preheat the grill and grease it.
6. Coat the fish fillets with lime juice, garlic powder, a pinch of salt and pepper.
7. Wrap a two beacon slice around each fish fillets.
8. Place each one of them in a piece of foil and fold it around it.
9. Grill them for 32 to 42 mins. Serve them warm with the peach and pepper salsa.
10. Enjoy.

Mediterrean Lunch Box Salad with Pita

Prep Time: 30 mins
Total Time: 30 mins

Servings per Recipe: 4
Calories   360.9
Fat   29.6 g
Cholesterol   50.7 mg
Sodium   894.7 mg
Carbohydrates   15.5 g
Protein   10.4 g

Ingredients

3 vine-ripe tomatoes, cut into chunks
1 medium red onion, sliced
1/2 seedless cucumber, cut into chunks
1 red bell pepper, seeded and cut into chunks
1 green bell pepper, seeded and cut into chunks
1 C. kalamata olive
1/4 C. flat-leaf parsley, chopped

1/2 lb. feta cheese
1/4 C. extra virgin olive oil
3 tbsp apple cider vinegar
1 tsp dried oregano
kosher salt & ground black pepper
pita bread

Directions

1. Get a large mixing bowl: Combine in it the veggies, olives, and parsley.
2. Add the feta cheese with oil, vinegar, oregano, and a pinch of salt. toss them to coat.
3. Heat the pita bread on the grill and serve them with the veggies salad.
4. Enjoy.

AMERICAN
Shrimp Flatbreads

🥣 Prep Time: 15 mins
🕐 Total Time: 30 mins

Servings per Recipe: 4
Calories 116.7
Fat 9.2 g
Cholesterol 17.9 mg
Sodium 330.1 mg
Carbohydrates 3.2 g
Protein 5.7 g

Ingredients

1/2 C. tomato sauce
2 C. Traditional Mashed Potatoes
1 tbsp milk
1/4 C. alfredo sauce
2 tsp cilantro, chopped
1/16 tsp salt
1 pinch ground pepper
4 pieces naan bread
16 pieces shrimp, peeled and deveined
1 tbsp extra virgin olive oil

1/8 tsp cumin
1/16 tsp salt
1 pinch ground pepper
2 pieces avocados
2 slices swiss cheese
2 slices American cheese

Directions

1. Before you do anything, preheat the oven to 350 F.
2. Place a large saucepan over medium heat. Combine in it the potatoes with milk. Heat them while stirring until they become creamy. Pour the mixture into a greased baking dish. Pour over it the alfredo sauce. Bake it for 8 to 12 min until it starts bubbling.
3. Garnish it with cilantro, a pinch of salt and pepper. Place it aside to cool down for a while.
4. Place a small pan over medium heat. Heat in it the oil.
5. Stir in it the shrimp with cumin, a pinch of salt and pepper.
6. Cook them for 3 to 5 min while stirring.
7. Slice the naan bread in half. Spoon to it the tomato sauce, avocado, mashed potato, grilled shrimp, American cheese and Swiss cheese.
8. Place the sandwiches on a baking sheet. Broil them in the oven for 3 to 4 min. Serve them warm.
9. Enjoy.

Italian Basil Bread

Prep Time: 10 mins
Total Time: 15 mins

Servings per Recipe: 4
Calories   125.1
Fat   13.1 g
Cholesterol   0.0 mg
Sodium   3.7 mg
Carbohydrates 2.1 g
Protein   1.0 g

Ingredients

- 15.5 inches loaf crusty Italian bread, cut into 12 slices
- 4 tbsp olive oil
- 4 tbsp basil pesto, see appendix
- 4 tbsp sun-dried tomato pesto

Directions

1. Place a grill pan over medium heat.
2. Coat the bread slices with oil.
3. Toast in it the bread slices for 2 to 3 min on each side. Transfer them to a serving plate.
4. Top them with basil pesto and tomato pesto. Serve them immediately.
5. Enjoy.

PUMPKIN
Grilled 101

Prep Time: 5 mins
Total Time: 15 mins

Servings per Recipe: 4
Calories   30.3
Fat   3.4 g
Cholesterol   0.0 mg
Sodium   290.8 mg
Carbohydrates   0.0 g
Protein   0.0 g

Ingredients

1 small pumpkin, sliced
1 tbsp olive oil
1 tbsp rosemary, chopped

1/2 tsp sea salt

Directions

1. Before you do anything, preheat the grill.
2. Coat the pumpkin slices with oil. Season them with rosemary and sea salt.
3. Grill them for 5 to 6 min on each side until they become soft. Serve them warm.
4. Enjoy.

Benny's
Backyard Beans

Prep Time: 5 mins
Total Time: 15 mins

Servings per Recipe: 4
Calories	10.7
Fat	0.0 g
Cholesterol	0.0 mg
Sodium	147.2 mg
Carbohydrates	2.4 g
Protein	0.5 g

Ingredients

1/2 lb. green Romano beans, ends trimmed
extra virgin olive oil

2 garlic cloves, minced
sea salt
pecorino romano cheese, grated

Directions

1. Place a grill pan over medium heat.
2. Toss the beans with a drizzle of olive oil. Season them with a pinch of salt.
3. Cook in it the beans for 3 to 4 min on each side.
4. Transfer them to a plate then top them with garlic, salt, and cheese. Serve them warm.
5. Enjoy.

HOW TO
Grill Hash Browns

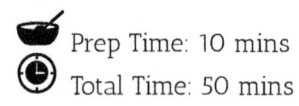

🥣 Prep Time: 10 mins
🕐 Total Time: 50 mins

Servings per Recipe: 4
Calories   570.4
Fat   49.5 g
Cholesterol   61.0 mg
Sodium   241.6 mg
Carbohydrates   31.9 g
Protein   3.8 g

Ingredients

- 4 tbsp olive oil
- 8 tbsp butter
- 1 (16 oz.) packages frozen hash browns
- 4 slices Monterey jack pepper cheese
- Toppings
- minced dried onion
- barbecue seasoning
- salt
- pepper

Directions

1. Before you do anything, preheat the grill and grease it.
2. Get four large pieces of foil. Top each one of them with 1 tbsp of olive oil and 1 tbsp of butter.
3. Divide half of the hash brown on them. Top them with cheese followed by the rest of the hash brown.
4. Top them with the remaining butter followed by dry onion, BBQ seasoning, a pinch of salt and pepper.
5. Gently pull the edges of foil to the middle and pinch them to seal them.
6. Grill the hash brown packets for 15 to 20 min on each side. Serve them warm.
7. Enjoy.

Printed in Great Britain
by Amazon